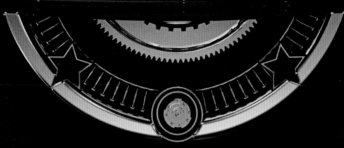

Text and photographs copyright © 2015 Back2Back Productions Ltd
Design and layout copyright © 2015 Carlton Books Ltd

This edition published by SevenOaks
20 Mortimer Street
London W1T 3JW

A CIP Catalogue record for this book is available from the British Library

ISBN 978 1 78177 258 4

Printed and Bound in Dubai

Editorial Manager: Roland Hall
Design: Russell Knowles
Picture Research: Paul Langan
Production: Rachel Burgess

CARS THAT ROCK

WITH BRIAN JOHNSON

**BURN RUBBER WITH BRIAN
IN THE MOST ICONIC
CARS EVER BUILT**

BY BRIAN JOHNSON
WITH **MARK DIXON**

SEVENOAKS

CONTENTS

FOREWORD

Mname is Brian Johnson and I sing in a band called AC/DC. Music is my life and always has been. But when the music stops, my greatest passion is motor racing.

As children, we all want to grow up to be a fighter pilot, a professional footballer, or even a rock 'n' roll singer. We fantasise about getting the girl and gaining the glory. Few, in my opinion, ascend to the rarefied atmosphere inhabited by the great racing drivers like Nuvolari, Fangio, Senna, Moss or McLaren.

This book is dedicated to all of you who share my secret desire to make a car go faster than anyone else's. We follow the same religion, you and I. We know that, when all's said and done, it's Cars That Rock.

Brian Johnson, 2015

ABOVE A victorious moment at the 2014 Mille Miglia with my co-author, Mark Dixon. We never had a cross word, and laughed for a thousand miles.

OPPOSITE My first date with a new love in my life, the Jaguar Project 7, at the Gaydon Jaguar/ Land Rover test track. If this car doesn't make you smile, then you're already dead.

1 | ALFA ROM

ONE OF THE MOST SIGNIFICANT GRAND PRIX CARS EVER MADE

EO

> ## " I'm one of very few people who has ever been allowed to drive the P3... "

One of the proudest moments of my life was reaching the top of the chart. Not the chart for album sales, but the one in the *Top Gear* studio with the lap times of each "Star in a Reasonably Priced Car". And then for the next 12 months, I sweated every Sunday when Jeremy Clarkson read out the latest Star in a Car's lap time. Who wants to be number two?

I was reminded of my day with the Stig when I visited the Autodromo di Modena, which – as you'll have guessed from the name – is a long way from the *Top Gear* test track in Surrey. I was there as a guest of the Italian motorway police, the Polizia Stradale, and to show me how they stop a suspect vehicle they set up a chase involving a mystery guy in a KTM X-Bow track car. He was wearing a helmet and I still don't have a clue who he was because, like the Stig, he never took it off. He could have been the Stig's Italian cousin, for all I know.

The motorway police in Italy use Alfa Romeos, as they have done since the 1950s, and it's a marque that suits their film star image. Is there anything cooler than an Italian motorway cop? With their sexy boots, purple-striped trousers, peaked caps and obligatory shades, they manage to look glamorous and intimidating at the same time. And you can't do that if you're driving a Hyundai.

Alfa Romeo is as much a part of Italian culture as the Trevi Fountain or Sophia Loren. The Romeo bit of the name comes from its founder, Nicola Romeo, while Alfa should really be written ALFA because it stands for Anonima Lombarda Fabbrica Automobili – which in

ABOVE The great Alfa Romeo driving police team, at Autodromo Di Modena. You do not want to pick a fight with these boys.

OPPOSITE ABOVE The Polizia Stradale Modena in full force.

OPPOSITE BELOW Two generations of Alfa Romeo highway patrol cars – eat your heart out, CHP!

LEFT Francesco Eroico explains how the latest Alfa sports car, the 4C, is manufactured, and it really *is* advanced.

BELOW With Francesco taking a closer look at the carbon-fibre chassis that makes the 4C so darn fast.

OPPOSITE A beautiful line-up of brand new 4Cs at the Maserati plant in Modena where Alfa Romeo now make their top-of-the-line cars.

whole lot better in Italian.

Without Alfa Romeo there would be no Ferrari, because Enzo Ferrari began his career with Alfa as a works racing driver. After the Second World War he set up his own car company – and we all know how that turned out. Alfa Romeo never produced supercars of the kind that Ferrari has made since the 1960s, but it has turned out some utterly gorgeous sporting machines. Recently it returned to the top table with the fabulous Ferrari-engined 8C super-coupé and, in 2013, the pocket-rocket 4C.

Because Alfa Romeo and Maserati are both owned by Fiat, the 4C is built at Maserati's wonderful facility in Modena, the town known as the home of Italian supercars – Ferrari is just down the road. I was curious as to why this part of Italy has been the source of so many amazing machines, so I asked a group of young men on the 4C production line. "*Passione!*" was the response. And it's the obvious answer. Italians have more "passione" for fast cars than any nation on earth.

The 4C is built like a supercar, with a carbon-fibre monocoque that makes it incredibly light at a little over 900kg. Even the glass has been made extra thin to shave off as much weight as possible. It has a turbocharged four-cylinder engine – 4C stands for "Four Cylinders" – which has also been cast in aluminium to keep it as light as possible. It's like an Italian Lotus, following the motto coined by Lotus founder Colin Chapman: "Add lightness".

one out, and fortunately Alfa Romeo has its own test track at Balocco in north Italy. The 4C project leader is Domenico Bagnasco, and he's brave enough to sit alongside me as I put the car through its paces.

Like a lot of modern performance cars, the 4C gives you a number of engine and handling settings to choose from. Alfa call it the "DNA" of the car, which is a contrived way of labelling the settings Dynamic, Normal, and All-Weather – and then they go and spoil all that cleverness by adding an extra one called Race. In Race mode, all the electronic driver aids are switched off so that you can hang the tail out as much as you like. No prizes for guessing which I've selected.

We zip out onto the track, and within just a few seconds I've fallen in love with this little baby. It's seriously quick – 0–60mph takes less than 4.5 seconds and it can crack 160mph – and it has a dual-clutch 'flappy paddle' gearbox that swaps cogs faster than you could ever do it yourself. And despite what I said earlier about hanging the back end out, it's so well balanced that it rarely gets out of shape, however careless you are with the throttle. Because it's mid-engined and because the carbon-fibre body means it's not just very light but also very stiff, on a track it just goes where you point it.

I adore this car. A little while after I drove it, I was rung up by a good friend in LA who had just seen one and wanted to know what I thought of it. I told him to buy one – but to wait a few months first. It seems that some dealers were slapping a 20,000-dollar premium on this

a grand car, because so many people wanted one. That's just greedy. Charging buyers a hefty whack on top of the purchase price is a good way for governments to rake in some income, however, which is why the Italians have always bought small-engined cars – they get taxed heavily on anything bigger than a 2-litre, and Italians hate paying taxes. Some of you may remember the Alfasud, the baby coupé that was sold in the UK during the 1970s. My sister Julie bought a secondhand one that was two years old. It went through one winter in the north-east before it rotted out.

The Alfasud was fitted with a little flat-four 'boxer' engine, which was a rare departure for Alfa. Usually it preferred a twin-cam four-cylinder, which went into dozens of different models from 1954 to 1994. The twin-cam is a jewel of a thing and one of the all-time classic designs. It was used in family cars, sports cars, racing cars – even four-wheel-drive jeeps. You don't actually need an all-alloy twin-cam engine with hemispherical combustion chambers in a 1950s jeep, but it's impossible to separate Alfa Romeo from its racing heritage. They had the engine, so they would use it.

You'll find versions of that engine in many of the most special race and rally cars from Alfa Romeo's competition history, which today are looked after by a club called Scuderia del Portello. It was started in the early 1980s – Scuderia is Italian for "team", and Portello is the district in Milan where Alfa used to have its factory – by a group of enthusiasts who wanted to use their historic Alfas rather than just park them up at car shows. Since the closure of Alfa's factory museum it's become the semi-official heritage arm of the company, and members race their cars all over the world.

When I visited the club's headquarters, they had invited a very special guest to meet me. Arturo Merzario looks more like an ageing rocker than I do, with his trademark cowboy hat, and you can tell he's lived a rock 'n' roll lifestyle – he was particularly taken with my TV crew's very pretty blonde assistant. In other words, he's pretty typical of an old racing driver. He was one of Alfa Romeo's stars during the 1960s and '70s. He raced in all kinds of series, from Touring Cars to

Formula 1, and he won some of the most prestigious events, such as the Targa Florio rally in Sicily.

Arturo and I chatted in front of an Alfa Romeo T33 racing car, an early version of the model in which he won the 1975 World Sports Car Championship. At least, I say "chatted": Arturo started off talking in English and then lapsed straightaway into Italian, while I just nodded my head and said "Si" at what I hoped were the right moments.

You'll see this happen a lot in *Cars That Rock*; my mother was Italian, but I can't speak it to save my life. There's a sequence where a lovely old boy called Emanuele, who used to be a race mechanic for the legendary Grand Prix driver Juan Manuel Fangio – world champion five times – is telling me about Fangio. He's speaking in rapid Italian that becomes more and more quickfire as his enthusiasm carries him away, and all the time I'm trying to look as if I have a clue about what he's saying, and hoping that I'm not grinning and nodding as he tells me how so-and-so died in a horrific accident.

But Arturo Merzario knows some English, and all of a sudden he says something that I have no problem understanding at all. "Eez very easy to drive. Why don'you try it?"

Ten seconds later I'm in the driving seat of one of the earliest Type 33 racing cars, with a 2-litre V8 behind me and the huge air intake that gives it the nickname Periscopica – literally, a periscope. Unfortunately there isn't a race track handy, so my drive will be a few laps of the village streets surrounding the Scuderia del Portello's clubhouse, complete with speed bumps every hundred yards. I do get a police escort, though, and where else but in Italy would the police let you take a full-house race car out onto the public road?

Needless to say, I can't get beyond second gear on those bumpy streets, and my left foot is soon swollen up like a football from the weight of the racing clutch. The windshield is also old and scratched, so that I can't see a thing with the sun in my eyes... But I'd love to try this car on a track. Driving in towns and cities is rarely much fun.

That reminds me: someone lent me a 1960s Alfa Duetto Spider – like the one driven by Dustin Hoffman in *The Graduate* – when we

OPPOSITE Me and the film crew pointing out the obvious ... at the Scuderia Del Portello (the famous Alfa Romeo enthusiasts club).

ABOVE LEFT Champagne to celebrate the end of filming.

ABOVE RIGHT Arturo Merzario, me, Marco Casani and my police escort. Or were the cops there to escort the wonderful Alfa Type 33? We certainly stopped traffic.

RIGHT Me and the Alfa racing legend that is Arturo Merzario. I thought he was the Lone Ranger.

LEFT Early morning start in Milan – the birthplace of Alfa Romeo.

BELOW I ask Michael, the director, when I am going to get paid. He just laughs.

OPPOSITE Getting ready to take the 1969 Alfa Romeo Spider Veloce for a spin around downtown Milan (maybe spin is not the right word – more like crawl). Crazy traffic.

were filming in Milan. We started at about 9.30 in the morning and word soon got out that "Brian Johnson of AC/DC" was in town, and people were everywhere taking pictures on their camera phones. By 11.30 it was on the social media websites that I was looking to buy a house in Milan!

For all of those frustrations, there are times that exceed your wildest expectations, and the highlight for me was getting to drive one of the greatest and most significant Grand Prix cars ever made: the 1932 Alfa Romeo P3, as piloted by Tazio Nuvolari in won of the greatest victories of his spectacular career. In 1935, he won the German Grand Prix in front of a huge German crowd and a group of high-ranking Nazis, beating all their high-tech, no-expense-spared Silver Arrow race cars in the process.

There's a great story that illustrates Nuvolari's singlemindedness. Like many racing drivers, he started his career with motorcycles, and during qualifying for the Monza Grand Prix he crashed his bike and broke both legs. The doctor set them in plaster and told him he wouldn't be able to walk for several weeks, let alone ride. But Nuvolari had his mechanics lash him onto his motorbike and hold him upright until the race began. He won the race.

When I went to the Balocco test track to drive the 4C, the people at

Alfa said they would bring their P3 out for me. It's so tremendously valuable that I was only expecting I'd get to see it and maybe touch it, and it wasn't until someone handed me an old-fashioned racing helmet – like a polo helmet – and told me to get in and put my foot on the clutch, that I started to realize what was about to happen. What made it all the more intimidating was that there was a big crowd of journalists there for the launch of the 4C. No pressure, then.

The Alfa Romeo P3 is powered by a twin-supercharged straight-eight, and to keep the car's centre of gravity as low as possible, the transmission splits into a pair of propshafts that fork in a Y-shape around the driver's seat. Even so, you sit up a lot higher than in a modern race car, and as I'm about to find out, going into the corners takes a bit of getting used to.

I slip on my shades in lieu of racing goggles, and a helpful mechanic inserts an electric starter into the end of the crankshaft. The glorious Alfa 2.9-litre eight-cylinder engine lights up instantly with a crisp rasp that's overlaid by the whir of the twin superchargers. Give it just a bit of gas, let the clutch in smoothly and I'm out onto the circuit, quickly gaining confidence as I realize that this Grand Prix car is not the slightest bit difficult to drive. It's a damn sight easier than my 1929 Bentley, that's for sure!

Two Alfa greats – on the left the glorious 1932 P3; on the right, the beautiful 2014 4C.

Faster and faster I go, hardly able to believe that I'm piloting the car driven by Nuvolari, one of my biggest heroes. The TV director has told me to describe what I'm feeling as I drive around, but for once in my life I don't want to say anything: I just want to live in the moment. I'm now circling at a goodly speed and I'm amused to discover how the slipstream will try to pull off your head if you let it stray outside the little box of dead air created by the tiny six-inch aeroscreen – you can feel the chinstrap of the helmet digging into your skin.

All too soon, of course, they're waving me in before I get over-confident and damage this priceless piece of Italian heritage, as important to the twentieth century as Michelangelo's David is to the sixteeenth. But, praise the Lord, the Italian sound engineer confesses that he forgot to switch his recording equipment on before I went out. Would I mind doing it again? Oh, hell, if I must...

I discover later that I'm one of very few people who has ever been allowed to drive the P3, and the others were ex-Formula 1 racers. The guys from Alfa trusted this old rock 'n' roll dude, and I'll never forget it. That's Italy; that's the passion. They're happy to share it with you if they know you feel the same way.

Even those motorway cops who we did the chase sequence with, following the KTM X-Bow, turned out to be fantastic fun. They are the people you never want to meet when you're on vacation – but after an afternoon with these guys I think I have a get-out-of-jail-free card on the highways of Italy for life. They were like a bunch of great kids.

The best bit was that one of them was a massive AC/DC fan, and he had 'Back In Black' blasting out of the PA speakers on his police car. Can you imagine that happening in Britain?

They still wouldn't let me have a gun, though.

LEFT Me and the legendary P3, which was driven to victory by Tazio Nuvolari (and I'm in his helmet!) I still have to pinch myself, in case it was a dream.

BELOW LEFT Stefano Agazzi, Alfa history expert, shows me the P3's innovative 8-cylinder engine. I stand back and admire the P3 (worth millions) before – miraculously – being allowed to drive it around the Alfa Romeo test track at Balocco; **BELOW** I was shaking when they said, "Brian, you driva." After this moment, there is no more wish list. I'm done.

OPPOSITE ABOVE Domenico Bagnasco, the project chief for the C4, shows me the business end of the their new baby, the best Alfa in ages.

OPPOSITE BELOW A very happy Mr Johnson – I am about to find out how fast this remarkable sports car can go.

2 | BENTLEY

THE SPIRIT OF THE BENTLEY BOYS

BENTLEY

> ❝ **My Bentley is agricultural but seductive. Like a Massey-Ferguson with tits and a nice smile.** ❞

George Best, the alcoholic but undeniably handsome footballer of the '60s and '70s, famously said: "I spent a lot of money on booze, birds and fast cars – the rest I just squandered."

I know plenty of people in the music business like that – not to mention the band – but few live that kind of life with the style exhibited by the Bentley Boys of the 1920s. This tight-knit band of brothers were the British "Rat Pack" of their day: extremely wealthy, charismatic and dedicated to racing motor cars without much thought about the consequences. They gave Bentley four straight wins at Le Mans in 1927–30, but never let motor racing get in the way of having fun.

Leader of the pack was Woolf Barnato. Immensely rich from his family's investment in South African gold and diamond mines, he not only put up the money to keep Bentley going in the 1920s but was also the company's star driver. He was tall, very good-looking and an all-round sportsman. He also liked women. A lot. One of his Bentley limousines – the one that was reserved for evening use – had a single seat for the driver, and the rest of the cabin arranged in an enclosed L-shape fashion with blinds over the windows to turn it into a rolling boudoir. Rock 'n' roll!

But the Bentley boys were brave men, too. Their generation had been through the horrors of the First World War, and anything that motorsport could throw up must have seemed like small beer in comparison. Even so, to get an idea of the kind of risks they were taking whenever they raced their Bentleys, you only need to visit a

ABOVE Me and Richard Charlesworth, head of Bentley Heritage, in front of W.O. Bentley's very own 8-litre beauty. Mr Bentley loved this car.

OPPOSITE Brian Gush shows me two fantastic racing Bentleys at their Crewe HQ: the white GT3 and the green, Le Mans-winning, Speed 8. They wouldn't let me buy either.

genteel corner of Surrey near the sleepy suburb of Weybridge. It's called Brooklands, and for a while it was the fastest racing circuit in the world.

Brooklands was an early example of a banked circuit, with the track elevated at a seemingly crazy angle in the long corners so that centrifugal force kept racing cars pressed down onto the concrete rather than flinging them into the surrounding trees. It was built in 1907 and closed during Second World War, after which it never reopened. What's left of it has been preserved by the Brooklands Trust, including a section of that infamous concrete banking.

Bentley and Brooklands were very closely associated during the 1920s, with Bentleys winning about half the races for which they were entered. You only have to watch old newsreel footage of those huge lorry-like cars thundering around the very top of the banking – where speeds were highest – to understand how dangerous it was. You can see the drivers, sitting upright in their tall machines, literally bouncing up and down like horseriders as they try to damp out the shocks being transmitted from the bumpy concrete surface.

Visit the banking today and it's even more surreal. You can't actually stand on the very top part of the track because the angle is too steep. No one can drive a car there now, either, because the concrete is too broken up by age. But, to my everlasting gratitude, I was allowed to get close to the top in a vintage Bentley when I visited for filming.

And not just any vintage Bentley, either. In 1929, "Bentley Boy" Tim Birkin raced a 4.5-litre Bentley in the Double-Twelve at Brooklands – and I was privileged to sit in the very same seat where he'd diced with death 85 years earlier. Birkin broke the lap record here twice, and clocked nearly 138mph on the bumpy banking. Incredible.

Rumbling onto that hallowed concrete meant all the more to me because I've been a vintage Bentley owner for about eight years. I bought a 4.5-litre from a well-known dealer in England and shipped it over to my home in Florida, where I drive it a lot. People respect it on the road – they have no idea what it is, but they appreciate its imposing demeanour. It's agricultural, but seductive. Kind of like a Massey-Ferguson with tits and a nice smile.

Even though I'm now a pretty experienced vintage Bentley driver, I still don't find it easy. The steering is really heavy at slower speeds and making a smooth gearchange is notoriously difficult with the Bentley crash gearbox. Every Bentley gearbox is different, but they're all tricky in varying degrees, and the person who says they never crunch a change in their 1920s Bentley is a liar. That said, the gearbox is incredibly tough and it's almost impossible to damage one, however much you mullah the changes.

The challenge is half the fun, though. Driving an old Bentley really is like piloting an old fighter plane. There's a mass of gauges sprinkled across the dashboard, with a rev counter the size of a soup plate directly in front of you and all kinds of devices unknown to today's drivers – a pump to pressurize the fuel tank, extra levers to set the throttle and adjust the ignition timing. And you go through a starting procedure like an aircraft from the Second World War: magnetos ON, fuel pump ON, ignition timing SET... then you press the starter button ... and the big Bentley motor rumbles into life.

Manhandling the famous Birkin Bentley at full throttle along the Brooklands banking is something that will stick with me forever. I don't mind admitting that my sphincter was twitching like a rabbit's nose as I put my foot down and soared towards the enticing upper edge of the track, now half-hidden by encroaching undergrowth, where so many drivers crashed and died. Among them was Clive Dunfee, one of the Bentley Boys, whose Le Mans-winning Speed Six put a wheel over the top, cartwheeled into the trees and totally disintegrated.

The car I drove at Brooklands was a 4.5-litre, but the one that everyone thinks of when you mention a vintage Bentley is the supercharged version, the so-called Blower Bentley. It was designed to give the extra speed needed to get ahead at Le Mans, but the fact is that the Blower Bentleys were never particularly successful. Those four Le Mans victories were taken by unsupercharged cars.

It was Tim Birkin who pushed to have the 4.5-litre engine supercharged; company founder Walter Owen (known as "WO") Bentley thought a bigger unblown engine was the answer – and was proved right when his new 6.5-litre Speed Six romped to victory at Le Mans in 1929 and 1930.

W.O. Bentley certainly knew his engines. During the First World War, he designed a new type of rotary engine for the Sopwith Camels used by the Royal Flying Corps. This had aluminium rather than cast-iron pistons, an innovation that WO had introduced when he was selling imported DFP cars before the war. Aluminium is lighter

than iron, so less energy was needed to make the pistons change direction inside the cylinders when they were moving up and down.

When he started making his own cars in 1919, the Bentley 3 Litre could boast four overhead valves for each of its four cylinders. Remember how much fuss there was about the 16-valve Golf GTi in the 1980s? Bentley was making 16-valve engines more than 60 years earlier.

The Bentley 3-Litre was the smallest and lightest of all Bentley's cars, but it was still a substantial piece of kit: what we used to call a "man's car". But women did race them, and still do, as I found out when I went to see a rather special Bentley 3-Litre with a uniquely feminine history.

Known as the Little Red Bentley for obvious reasons, this 3 Litre has the honour of being the first Bentley ever to be supercharged. Its then owner, a feisty female racer called May Cunliffe, had a Roots-type blower fitted during a major rebuild in 1926–27, following an accident. It must have been a big accident because May was not only badly injured but banned from racing for a year.

May didn't keep the Bentley very long – she took up flying in the 1930s – but after a chequered history with lots of different owners it now belongs to the classic car-loving Singer family, and is regularly

Rachel Singer
and if she lets them
Adam Singer
Joe Singer

ABOVE LEFT With Bentley-mad Singer family, Joe, Rachel and Adam.

ABOVE RIGHT Rachel and I chat about women driving in the old days. They were against the men and there was no pity for titty.

LEFT Rachel and I head out, with the names of the car's drivers on the bonnet of this beautiful Bentley Blower 3 Litre.

BELOW On the road. Boy, this girl could drive.

OPPOSITE We make it back (just). A very fast van scraped the side of the car.

raced by Rachel Singer, a petite and rather attractive blonde lady. No prizes for guessing what I said when Rachel asked if I wanted to go out for a drive.

You might think that bright red paint on a vintage Bentley would look horribly vulgar, dear boy, but because this one has a really short chassis and a truncated racing tail, it works surprisingly well. There's a massive single carburettor that tries valiantly to let enough fuel into the mixture being force-fed by the supercharger, and at a relatively mild state of boost the four-cylinder engine is giving around 100bhp. That may not sound like a huge amount, but it's enough to push this relatively light car to the magic "ton".

Rachel handles the Little Red Bentley with real skill and confidence, always making allowance for the fact that it doesn't have brakes on the front wheels, like a lot of early 3 Litres. You do feel very exposed sitting upright and unprotected in this 100mph racer, the cheeks on your face being pulled into Hall of Mirror shapes by the blast of the slipstream and your ears assaulted by the blaring of the drainpipe-sized exhaust. I try not to remember that the very first owner of this car was killed in 1925 while practising for a race in it.

No one's sure whether the Little Red Bentley was fitted with the supercharger at Bentley's workshop or somewhere else, but WO himself is known to have been vigorously opposed to supercharging.

He famously declared that "to supercharge a Bentley engine was to pervert its design and corrupt its performance". Sadly for him, the result of having to seek financial backing from Woolf Barnato meant that he had less and less say in how the company was run as the 1920s progressed – and then came the Depression of 1929. Bentley's glory days were over.

The ultimate insult was that, when Bentley went bust in 1931, it was taken over by the company's bitter rival, Rolls-Royce. W.O. himself was given a token position as a technical adviser, but his contract wasn't renewed after 1935. The buggers at Rolls-Royce even took back his own beloved Bentley 8 Litre saloon, and WO had nothing more to do with the cars that bore his name from then until his death in 1971.

Rolls-Royce moved Bentley production to their own factory in Derby and then just after World War Two to another plant in Crewe, where they had been making Merlin aero engines during the war. And that's where Bentleys are still made today, following the sale of the company to the mighty VW Group in 1998.

VW invested a huge amount of money in the Crewe factory but thankfully they respected the history of the site and have updated it without simply knocking it all down and starting again. If you go there today, you can still see the classic saw-tooth factory roofs, which are aligned north-south to pull in maximum light, and some of

the old buildings in which Merlins were tested before they were fitted into Spitfires, Hurricanes and Lancasters. Until just a few years ago, there were even remains of WW2 camouflage on the brick walls.

They still make 12-cylinder engines at Crewe, but instead of mighty Merlin V12s the workforce now produces W12 powerplants, not just for Bentley but for the whole VW Group. When I visited in 2014, Crewe had already built 70,000 of them – not so much coals to Newcastle as W12s to Wolfsburg. Bentley puts the twin-turbo W12 into its gorgeous Continental GT Coupé, and I know it's gorgeous because I had one for a couple of years until I was seduced away by a Rolls-Royce, as you'll read elsewhere in this book. Sorry, W.O.

In cooking form, the W12 puts out a mere 567bhp, but in the flagship of the range, the Continental GT Speed, that's raised to 626bhp. Officially, the Speed has a top, er, speed of 205mph – but people in the know say it's considerably more. As I found out when I went to a

top-secret testing facility in the heart of the English countryside, for a few driving tips from one of Britain's greatest ever racers.

Derek Bell, MBE, made a name for himself in endurance racing by winning the Le Mans 24 Hours five times, the 24 Hours of Daytona three times, and the World Sportscar Championship twice. Since retiring from professional racing in 2000, he's been an ambassador for Bentley – so who better to put me through my paces in a new Speed?

Millbrook Proving Ground is unique in the British Isles in having a two-mile circular track which is banked, like Brooklands, so that test drivers can stay flat-out for hours at a time. With me behind the wheel of the new Speed – all quilted leather and figure-hugging seats – Derek coaxes me to gradually put my foot down and move up to the most steeply banked part of the five-lane circuit. The Bentley W12 is smooth as a gravy sandwich as we hit 140, 145 and finally 150mph, which is a long way short of the car's maximum speed

but feels pretty damn fast when you're taking what is basically an endless corner.

Then Derek shows me Millbrook's party trick. "Lose a little speed and just drift down into the lane below," he says. I obey the master. "Now, take one hand off the wheel." Feeling a little confused, I lift my left hand off the steering wheel. "And now the other". Whaat? You want me to take both hands off the steering wheel at 100mph? Oh well, he must know what he's doing. I lift my right hand up, so I'm holding both hands well clear of the wheel rim – and the Speed continues to run absolutely true, the geometry of the track combining with the laws of physics to hold it with inch-perfect precision in the exact centre of our lane.

Dapper Derek, of course, is cool as a cucumber – and not just because the Bentley's air conditioning is gently massaging our temples – but when I mention that I've driven on the banking at Brooklands he admits that the prospect of racing there would have utterly terrified him. "They really were heroes," he agrees. "Up here we have guard rails. They didn't. I can't imagine what it was like to race somebody,

knowing I was on the limit, and that if I went off then I was dead.

Heroes, indeed. For me, these lines by poet Christopher Logue sum up the spirit of the Bentley Boys better than I ever could:

> Come to the edge.
> We might fall.
> Come to the edge.
> It's too high!
> COME TO THE EDGE!
> And they came,
> And we pushed,
> And they flew.

OPPOSITE Without front-wheel brakes, piloting the 3-litre on narrow country lanes is plenty exciting.

BELOW Racing legend Derek Bell and I in front of the Bentley Continental GT Speed at Millbrook proving ground. Derek is the perfect ambassador for Bentley and is a cool dude.

3 | BUGATTI

THE SUPERCAR YOU CAN DRIVE WITH ONE FINGER

BUGATTI

Fourteen radiators. Let me say that again. Fourteen radiators. We didn't have that many at the school I went to in Dunston, in north-eastern England – and it gets bloody cold in the north-east. But that's how many radiators there are in a single Bugatti Veyron.

Everything about the Veyron is extraordinary. It's the car for which the word "superlative' could have been invented; the car that would be the ace in any game of Top Trumps. It costs in the region of £2 million pounds to buy, yet if you add up all the development costs, then it loses the makers some £4 million for every car sold. It's completely bonkers – but I love the fact that the Volkswagen Group, which owns Bugatti, has the *cojones* to throw away such huge amounts of money just so it can say it produces the best road car in the world.

I'll admit, I've thought about buying a Veyron. Not a new one, obviously. What do you think I am – made of money? What stops me, though, is the fact that you never own a Veyron. The car owns you.

Let me give you a few examples. The tyres have to be replaced every 6,000 miles or every year, or Bugatti gets very upset. That costs 18 grand. Then the wheels have to be changed every three years. That's another £35,000. Every time you take the key out of the ignition, electronic data is sent by satellite to the factory, so they can see how you've been driving. Every year you have to give it back to them for upgrades – which start at £40,000. And if you don't do it, they'll wipe their hands of you. What happens if I go on tour for two years?

But it is an amazing car. And the place where it's made is amazing, too. All the parts are manufactured elsewhere – the bodyshell is

OPPOSITE ABOVE Two slightly famous legends parked up at the Cité De L'Automobile in Mulhouse, France (Bugatti's home town).

OPPOSITE BELOW The Bugatti's noisy bit, and wallet emptier.

BELOW Rain stops play – this is the closest I got to driving a 1937 Bugatti Type 57 Atalante. It was too expensive to risk in the rain! Double bollocks!

> ## " You never own a Bugatti Veyron. The car owns you. "

made in Germany, and the gearbox comes from Bristol, of all places – before being shipped to Molsheim in Southern France, where they are assembled into Veyrons by a team of just 10 technicians. They use titanium bolts to hold the big bits together, and you won't be surprised to hear that each bolt costs several hundred euro – and they can be used only once before they have to be discarded and recycled.

Bugatti doesn't have anything so vulgar as a factory to make its cars, of course. Instead it has an *atelier*, which is French for "artisan workshop" and is in the grounds of the château that was once owned by Ettore Bugatti, who founded the company. It's deliberately been built in an oval shape like the outline of the Bugatti badge, so that customers can recognize it when they arrive in their helicopters and private jets.

A private jet would probably lose out in the acceleration stakes to a Veyron, which in Super Sport spec takes just 2.7 seconds to get to 60mph from rest. So when I visited Molsheim, it was only proper that we went to a nearby airstrip to see if I could beat my personal Johnson land speed record of 208mph, which I set on the banking at Daytona Raceway, in Florida.

To get there, we drove, of course. The truly remarkable thing about the Veyron is how user-friendly it is on the road. For a start, when you first set eyes on it in the metal rather than in pictures, it's a lot smaller than you expect. It doesn't even look that sporty inside, either. The dashboard is almost simple; it's not covered in dials and switches like a vintage car's, like my 1920s Bentley or my 1940s MG TC. But now let me throw a few Veyron statistics at you. 1,200 horsepower. 1,500

LEFT The Mulhouse auto museum. It is the world's largest collection of Bugattis – they have even more then the Saudi royal family.

BELOW Richard Keller, the Mulhouse Museum chief curator, shows me another one.

OPPOSITE And another one ... You must visit this place – it's unbelievable.

N m of torque. Ten VW Golf engines (that's how many are needed to produce the 1,500 N m of a single Veyron engine). And one finger.

Now, the finger is not what passers-by give you when you drive a Veyron. People actually love it. One finger is all you need to steer a Veyron at normal speeds, because it's such an easy car to drive. You can leave the gearbox in Automatic and pootle around as if you're in a Prius. And because the Veyron is not that big, by modern standards – it's just under an inch wider than a 1980s Ferrari Testarossa, but it's also an inch shorter – it doesn't feel unwieldy on country roads.

That's just as well, because I'm sitting next to the man who set the world speed record for a production car, Pierre-Henri Raphanel. In 2010, at Volkswagen's test track in Germany, he pushed a Veyron Super Sport to 267.8mph. The car we're in today is a Veyron Grand Sport Vitesse, which is the open version, and that holds the record for an open-top car at a mere 254.04mph.

Pierre-Henri is a lovely guy, with a wonderful French accent. When we get to the airstrip, we have to share the runway with three planes that are waiting to take off. So I'm sitting behind this Cessna – in a Veyron – and Pierre-Henri says to me: "Ve must whet for permiss-y-on from ze tower. Zen, when I say gew, you put ze foot on ze accelerateur and you just go fasta, fasta, fasta."

"But where do I stop?" I ask. "This runway looks awful short and there's no braking point."

"I vill say to yew, 'Brakke brakke brakke!' and ven I say to yew, 'Brakke brakke brakke!', then you must brakke," replies Pierre-Henri. So that's what I do – only I can't help myself changing gear with the flappy paddles, instead of just leaving the car to take care of itself as Pierre-

Henri has instructed, and then I brake too early because I think I hear him telling me to "brakke" before he actually does so. Johnson fail.

The next run is better, but the airstrip is too short for the Veyron to get anywhere near its maximum speed, and I don't quite make 200mph. The Johnson land speed record is safe. It's one of the most exhilarating, amazing experiences I've ever had, though, and so can you if you have a couple of million quid to spare. Me? I think I'd rather spend the money on a 1920s Bugatti Type 35.

I've long fantasized about driving a Type 35, and I finally got the chance when I visited Molsheim, to see the Veyrons being made. Molsheim is where Ettore Bugatti set up shop in 1909, and when VW decided they were going to make the Veyron they bought Bugatti's old villa and built a little hi-tech atelier in the grounds. They even restored the villa to exactly how it was in Bugatti's time. Now that's cool.

Bugatti has a Type 35 in its collection and it's a proper car, a bit bashed around and not all shiny and pampered. This is the model that really put Bugatti on the map. It dominated Grand Prix racing in the 1920s, and it's one of Ettore's most successful designs. Wealthy gentlemen racers would spend their weekends racing Type 35s all over Europe, and on Monday the papers would be full of news of their victories.

If you think alloy wheels were invented in the 1960s, then think again, because the Type 35 has some of the grooviest spoked alloys you'll ever see. The car I'm driving is the 35T model, which means it has a gorgeous little straight-eight, but the ultimate version was the supercharged 35B. Put some methanol racing fuel into one of those puppies and you get 200bhp in something that weighs little more than a go-kart.

People always say that the Bugatti straight-eight sounds like tearing calico when you fire it up. Now, I can't remember the last time I even saw a piece of calico, let alone ripped it in two, but I can see what they're getting at: the eight-cylinder motor makes a fizzing, rasping sound when you rev it, turning into a rousing blare when you really give it some throttle.

First, though, we have to escape the modern industrial parks and housing developments that have sprung up around Bugatti's beautiful old 1920s villa. My co-pilot is Julius Kruta, from Bugatti Tradition, which looks after its old cars. He went to boarding school in England, don'cha know, so he speaks better English than I do, and he points out some of the sights as we negotiate endless roundabouts and head out to the countryside.

"There's the house Bugatti lived in... and here is the old factory," Julius calls out above the rush of the slipstream. "Ettore was well respected by his workers because he could do all the jobs that they did. The only thing he wasn't good at was making money – he always spent more than he earned, even in the good times."

Ettore Bugatti was a talented man, alright, but so was the rest of his family. His father, Carlo, made stylish and futuristic furniture. His brother, Rembrandt, was a skilled sculptor, particularly of animals, and son Jean proved a brilliant designer of coachwork for Ettore's car chassis. But the family would be dogged by tragedy. Rembrandt committed suicide in 1916, and Jean was killed in 1939 while testing a Bugatti Le Mans racer on the road near the factory – they say he swerved to avoid a drunken bicyclist, and crashed into a tree. Those trees still line the road just outside today's factory at Molsheim.

There are some great stories about Ettore. His attention to detail was legendary and he once wrote to his daughter Lydia, suggesting that if she wanted to continue working for the Bugatti company, then she'd better improve the style of the "L" and the "y" in her signature! He even designed the hinges for the oak doors of his factory, and had a special doorlatch made so that when he was riding though the works on horseback, his horse could lift it up with her nose and he didn't have to dismount...

But now we're clear of the Molsheim suburbs and Julius is encouraging me to give the Type 35 some stick. I've been frightened about overrevving it, but Julius urges me not to hold back: "You don't understand, Brian – this is a proper racing car, which won Grands Prix. You won't break it." He tells me I'm safe to rev it to 6,700rpm, which is a hell of a lot for a car this age, but then the engine is sweet as a nut, and boy, is this car quick! You have to work at it more than my Bentley – you have to pressurize the fuel tank by jiggling a hand pump every so often – but it's such a rewarding car to drive. The steering is so accurate, and the gears snick in tidily every time; it's much more manageable than the Bentley.

I could have gone home happy after driving the Type 35, but an hour up the road is a place with a lot more Bugattis – more than 120 of them, in fact. The Cité de l'Automobile is housed in an old textile factory that was once owned by two brothers, Fritz and Hans Schlumpf, who were fanatical about cars, and in particular Bugattis. They started collecting them in the 1950s and bought literally hundreds of them, which they stashed away in the old factory. Unfortunately they didn't spend the same kind of money on their workers' wages, and when the disgruntled proletariat found out about the collection, they occupied the place and forced the Schlumpf brothers into exile.

Now the "Schlumpf Collection" is France's national motor museum and open to the public. It's a staggering sight, with more than four hundred cars from 90 different marques illuminated by 900 Art Nouveau style cast-iron lamp posts. But I'm here to see the

Bugattis, and just one Bugatti in particular. Possibly the greatest car ever made, in every sense of the word.

Ettore Bugatti's company produced roughly 8,000 cars, every one of them a work of beauty, but his most fabled creation is the Royale. It was a car that reflected his personality – a car that was larger than life. They didn't have rock stars in the 1920s, but no-one had told Ettore that. When he rolled up somewhere in his Royale, wearing his big hat, the kings, queens, dukes and duchesses would all mutter to themselves, "Oh, Christ". And he'd always end up in the middle of the official line-up. Always.

At the time he designed the Royale, the biggest Rolls-Royce you could buy had a 7.7-litre engine. Ettore's Royale had a straight-eight of 14.7 litres. The chassis was more than 20 feet long, and the bonnet alone accounted for about half that. When you see a man standing alongside a Royale, he looks strangely shrunken, as if he's just had a snifter with Alice in Wonderland.

Ettore planned to build two-dozen Royales and flog them to the crowned heads of Europe and beyond, but the economic situation of the 1930s meant that, in the end, only six were made. Two of them are in the Schlumpf Collection, including the prototype, which was Ettore's own car. And I was allowed to sit behind the wheel – something which involved climbing over a ring of infra-red alarm beams that encircle the car, like The Pink Panther. Me, I was Inspector Clouseau (yes, I set off the alarm).

But it was worth it. "Lord, take me now!" I thought. "I'm ready!" The last time a Royale was sold, it's rumoured to have fetched €36 million. It makes the Veyron look positively cheap.

The ironic thing is that, while the Royale was a sales disaster, it helped save Bugatti from going bankrupt in the 1930s, because a batch of unused Royale engines were put into self-propelled railcars and sold to the French railway network. In the end, about 90 Bugatti railcars were built and they were very successful, apart from having horrendous fuel consumption – each engine did 2.5 miles to the gallon.

The railcars lasted longer than Bugatti itself did, because Ettore died in 1947 and his company stopped making cars soon after. There was a 1990s revival, when the four-wheel-drive EB110 supercar was produced, but it was not until the Veyron appeared in 2005 that the Bugatti name was really put back on the map.

Talking of names, the Veyron is a tribute to racing driver and French resistance hero Pierre Veyron, who won the 1939 Le Mans 24 Hours in a Type 57S – the last significant race win for Bugatti. It's an inspired choice for an inspiring car. Driving the Veyron was one of the most intense experiences I've ever had in my life; I'd have to pilot a fighter jet to get anywhere close to it again.

I wonder what Ettore Bugatti would say if he came down from heaven and saw a Veyron. I guess he'd look it over and see if he could do anything to improve it – and then he'd give up. Job done, Ettore, my lad. You can rest easy.

4 FORD VS CH

WEAPONS-GRADE SPEED MACHINES FOR MEN WITH BIG BALLS

HEVY

FORD vs CHEVY

> **Tip 1: turn the ignition on. Tip 2: hit the gas. Tip 3: don't hit the wall around the track.**

Unless you were born in the USA (now there's an idea for a song), it's hard to understand just how seriously Americans take the whole Ford versus Chevy thing. You can forget Ferrari versus Lamborghini – that's like two girls pushing each other in a playground. When it comes to their two homegrown brands, the Americans have taken competitiveness to an entirely new level. Just try Googling it. You'll find more than 20 million hits for Ford vs Chevy. There was even a Playstation game called just that.

In Britain, the closest we have is Ford versus Vauxhall, because Vauxhall is kind of a British version of Chevrolet – but the rivalry there is mostly between company car drivers obsessing about whether they have an "L" or a "GL" on their bootlid. In America, they take things more seriously. To misquote Liverpool manager Bill Shankly, it's not a matter of life or death – it's much more serious than that. Ford vs Chevy is like the North against the South, the Yankees fighting the Confederates, the Blue against the Grey.

Fords and Chevys are working-men's cars, and to a working man the car he drives is as important as the beer he drinks or the football team he supports. His livelihood depends on it. This passion spills over into motorsport, and the bluecollar battlegrounds are the banked oval circuits of NASCAR, where good ol' boys have been making dreams come true for half a century.

NASCAR stands for National Association of Stock Car Automobile Racing, and originally the cars were just that – "stock" cars that

ABOVE Rick Hendricks' private collection of cars – in Charlotte, North Carolina. Incredible.

OPPOSITE ABOVE Behind the wheel of Humpy Wheeler's 1939 Ford Coupe. An unbelievably nimble drive.

OPPOSITE BELOW Junior Johnson, the "Last American Hero", meets another Johnson. This man is a delight to talk to, and a true legend.

LEFT At some point this heavily customized creature was a 1970 Chevy Camaro Z28.

OPPOSITE ABOVE Marvin Panch, Daytona Beach stock car racing legend and I have a beer, or two. I could talk to him all day long. A wonderfully humble man.

OPPOSITE, BELOW LEFT Marvin and I pose for a photo.

OPPOSITE, BELOW RIGHT I try to do a piece to camera at the famous Turn 42 location on Daytona Beach, but the weather decides otherwise.

could have been driven straight off the showroom floor and raced. They're very different now: weapons-grade speed machines that hurtle round the track just inches apart at 200mph for hours on end. Way more drivers have been killed in NASCAR since it was founded in 1947 than in Formula 1. It's an incredibly demanding sport, and you need massive balls to take part.

I've always been a fan of Formula One but it wasn't until I moved to Florida that I started getting interested in NASCAR. What's the appeal, I wondered, in watching cars go round and round a circuit that doesn't have any proper corners? Why is it practically a religion to so many Americans?

To understand NASCAR, you have to go right back to the days of moonshine. In the southern states of America, the locals have always made their own alcohol, and the authorities have always tried to stop them. That's how moonshine got its name: it's homemade whiskey that's been distilled, in secret, at night by the light of the moon. During the years of Prohibition in the 1920s and early '30s, there was a great black market for this homemade booze, and it would be transported at night down country roads to the clubs and speakeasies in the towns and cities.

The guys who drove these cars had to be handy behind a wheel, because often the "Feds" would give chase and try to arrest them. They used big old sedans that could carry plenty of illicit booze, and they hotted up the engines to cope with the extra weight. Soon they started racing each other, too, on dirt roads and in fields, and it wasn't long before small-town businessmen started organizing local race meets and charging people to watch them.

In 1947, a particularly astute businessman called Bill France realized that the sport would only grow if it was officially regulated

and promoted – so he founded NASCAR. It really took off during the 1950s and by the '60s the old dirt tracks were being replaced with huge concrete stadiums capable of seating over 100,000 spectators. The Daytona International Speedway can seat twice as many people as Newcastle United's home ground at St James's Park. Hell, it has more seats than Wembley Stadium. And Daytona is a long way from being the biggest in NASCAR.

But while Daytona, Florida is now the home of NASCAR, many of the sport's top racers come from the state of North Carolina, which was prime moonshine country. And that's where I met a true legend of both moonshine and NASCAR, Junior Johnson.

Junior's life story reads like a film – which is why they made one based on his life, starring Jeff Bridges. It was called *The Last American Hero* after Junior's nickname, on account of how he started running moonshine for his daddy, served time in jail, then found his vocation as one of the most successful – what Americans call the "winningest" – NASCAR drivers of all time. He won 50 races before his retirement in 1966, and he invented the technique known as drafting, which means using a faster car's slipstream to give you a free tow so you can slingshot past them on the final lap.

I met Junior on a freezing cold day in winter, but I was instantly warmed by his soft Southern accent that rolls over you like honey. It's hard to believe that Junior, who is now well into his 80s and looks like your favourite granddad, was often involved in high-speed pursuits by the Feds as a teenager, but he was – "and they never caught me!" he insists.

I ask him whether it's true that he invented the famous bootlegger's turn: hauling a car through 180° to avoid a roadblock. "It's true, but I wrecked about four or five cars before I got it right!" he chuckles.

The Revenue would throw a spiked belt across the highway, so I had to learn how to turn around before hitting it and shredding my tyres."

Junior was 14 when he started running moonshine and he got sent to prison after being ambushed by the Feds as he was firing up his dad's whiskey still at four in the morning. When he came out of jail, 19 months later, he took up racing again. Like many bootleggers, Junior liked Fords, because they had a powerful V8 engine that was ideal for making a fast getaway. He wasn't alone in that – gangsters John Dillinger and Clyde Barrow (of Bonnie and Clyde fame) both sent letters to Henry Ford praising his V8.

When we were filming Junior for *Cars That Rock*, his long-time NASCAR buddy "Humpy" Wheeler kindly lent us a 1938 Ford V8 Coupe, very much like the ones that Junior used to escape from the Feds. But I had a shock when I opened the bonnet – inside there's a modern Chevy Corvette engine! How ironic is that. Fact is, though,

that racers (and moonshiners) didn't really care what car they drove. It's the race fans, and the guys who drive pick-up trucks, who fuel the flames of the Ford versus Chevy rivalry.

While Ford and Chevrolet, the companies, have been at each other's throats for decades, the man who gave his name to Chevrolet – Louis Chevrolet, a Swiss-born racing driver and engineer who came to America in 1901 – had his greatest success making go-faster Fords. Louis Chevrolet wasn't the greatest businessman and within four years of founding his company in 1911 he'd been sidelined by his partner. In later life he had some success making hotted-up Model T Fords but that all went pearshaped and he ended up, so the story goes, as an anonymous worker on the shop floor of a Chevrolet factory. He died penniless in 1941.

Henry Ford, on the other hand, became richer than God by introducing mass-production and selling more cars more cheaply

ABOVE LEFT Doug Douchardt, GM of Hendricks Motor Sports, the winningest NASCAR team, gives me the tour of their immaculate works.

LEFT and **ABOVE RIGHT** Chevy Generation 6 NASCAR bodies.

OPPOSITE The Hendricks' engine "delivery room/Dream Factory".

than anyone else. At one time roughly half the world's cars were made by Ford. He was a mass of contradictions: on the one hand he paid his workers well, and treated African American people the same as whites; on the other he was a control freak who had company spies check up on his employees' private lives, and hired thugs to beat people up trade union organizers. He died a multi-millionaire in 1947.

The Ford Motor Co brought out their first V8 way back in 1932, and it took more than 50 years for Chevrolet to respond. But when they did, in 1955, they came in with a bang. The small-block Chevy V8 became one of the most prolific V8 engines of all time, with more than 100 million produced right into the twenty-first century. And Chevrolet started winning on the racetracks. It's won more than twice as many NASCAR championships as Ford, with a dozen straight victories in the early 2000s.

To see how they do it, I visited the workshops of Hendrick Motorsports, just a mile from Charlotte Motor Speedway in North Carolina. In fact, the word "workshops" is misleading because it's a huge facility – they call it a campus – immaculately clean, and as impressive as McLaren's in its own way. But whereas McLaren comes across as a bit impersonal and robotic, Hendricks is all old-fashioned Southern charm and down-to-earth friendliness. Here I watched "Bear" – a huge man with a beard – torqueing the main caps down on a Chevy V8. He has the right name for the job.

Hendrick has 200 engines going through their 'shop at any one time, and they are assembled to the highest standards, without a computer in sight. This is old-school racing. When I met them, the Hendrick guys were adjusting to a new set of regulations which will see the engines restricted to 725bhp instead of the 850bhp they were allowed to produce up till then. But they weren't too upset. They'll

come up with new ways to get one over on the opposition. As they say in NASCAR, "It ain't cheatin'. It's creative thinkin'."

The two cars I find myself standing between a little while later, on the apron of the huge Charlotte Motor Speedway, are the last-generation full-fat jobs, each with the thick end of 900bhp to play with. One is a Chevrolet Impala SS, the other a Ford Fusion. And I'm blowed if I can tell them apart. But that's kind of the point, as champion NASCAR driver Randy LaJoie explains to this confused Geordie.

"To keep the racing close, NASCAR doesn't want one make to have a significant advantage over the other, so it allows only a small window of opportunity," he tells me. "These cars have engines that each produce the same horsepower. They look pretty similar on the inside, too, because they're governed by the same safety regulations about roll-cages and so on."

Randy is going to let me try both cars around the Charlotte speedway. Eeny-meeny-miny-mo – grab the Ford and out we'll go.

Helmet on, HANS neck brace on, slide into the racing seat through the open window like a true Duke of Hazzard. That's not to look cool; it's because these cars don't have doors. They are "silhouette" race cars, with lightweight metal shells over tubular spaceframe chassis, like full-size versions of radio-controlled plastic models. Even the headlights and front grilles are just stickers.

I can't believe how much space there is in here! It's just like sitting in a ballroom compared with most race cars. It's basic as basic can be; there's a row of gauges in front of me, but Randy says the best drivers hardly look at them. Can you give me any tips on how to do this, Randy?

"Tip One – turn the ignition on. Tip Two – hit the gas. Tip Three – don't hit the wall that runs around the track. And Tip Four – bring yourself a bucketful of balls."

With Randy's words of advice ringing in my ears, I flick the ignition on and push the button. *Ga-roarrrr!* It's like I've just kicked a T-Rex in the goolies. This thing is *loud*, and when I prod the throttle it responds with a vicious snarl, as if daring me to provoke it further. It sounds utterly evil.

There's a four-on-the-floor manual gearshift, but it's only there to get me up to speed; you don't change down for the corners in NASCAR, not when you're closing on them at 180mph. It's a surreal experience. These cars are set up to turn left all the time, so to keep going in a straight line you actually have to steer right – but then, when you enter the banked curve, you move your hands back to the centre and the car hunkers down and goes round beautifully. You can't believe this big lump of a thing isn't going to fly off the track, but it just sticks there. Unbelievable.

It's fitting that I drove this NASCAR Ford and Chevy at Charlotte, because the first ever race in what is now the Sprint Cup series – the ultimate NASCAR championship – took place here in 1949. Some 700 drivers have called North Carolina home, including the most winningest racer ever, who still lives here – and I got to meet him.

Richard Petty is nicknamed the King, and he truly is NASCAR

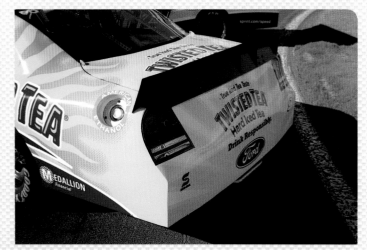

OPPOSITE Randy LaJoie gives me some sage advice –"Just bring big balls".

ABOVE Just about to get suited and booted for the Chevy.

ABOVE RIGHT The bootylicious end of the Ford.

RIGHT I climb the Charlotte Motor Speedway banking (without the aid of Sherpas or climbing boots, I might add).

BELOW "It's this big," I say, in front of the Ford Fusion. I'm talking about the engine.

ABOVE "King" Richard Petty's car collection in Level Cross, North Carolina. The king is much larger than life, with a kindness and charisma to match.

LEFT The 1969 Ford Torino that King Richard won his 100th title in. He went on to win an extraordinary 200 titles!

OPPOSITE Another superb car wins my affections – the first American car ever to do so: the new Petty Ford Mustang. Richard hands me the keys to the first one off their production line.

royalty, with 200 race victories and seven championships under his belt. He looks like a steam-punk gunslinger: tall and rangey, wearing black shades, a black leather jacket, and the most elaborate Stetson I've ever seen. He became a racer, he says, because his dad was one, and in those days and in these parts you tended to follow your dad into the family business.

"Racing was the South's sport. We didn't have professional football or basketball back then. My dad read in the paper that Bill France was holding a race meeting, so he borrowed a car, and that's how it all started."

Richard gives me the best summary of the whole Ford versus Chevy rivalry that I've yet heard.

"In the old days, there were no celebrity drivers. The advertising was all about Ford against Chevrolet, or Chevrolet against Plymouth or whatever. Then some of the drivers started getting famous, and the situation turned around. Now it's so-and-so against someone else, and they just happen to drive a Ford."

While I'm at Richard's office, he tells me to close my eyes because he has a surprise for me. He leads me out back to the workshop, and when I'm allowed to open them again, there in front of me is one of the most beautiful cars I've ever seen. It's finished in Petty Racing's trademark baby blue with a black roof and black-tinted windows, and it's clearly based on a new Ford Mustang, but it's been tweaked in lots of subtle ways. There's a NASCAR rear spoiler, racing brakes and race suspension, and a custom interior. I absolutely love it.

"This," says Richard, "is the prototype limited-edition Richard Petty Mustang. It's supercharged to 625 horsepower."

To cut a long story short, I end up buying one. It's not built yet, but it will be chassis 001, and I rather fancy having it shipped to England. Can you imagine how it would go down somewhere like the wilds of Somerset? "'Ere, our David, what be that spaceship that just went past?" "Oh, don't you be frettin' yoursel,f our Dad, that be just Brian in his Mustang."

So that's three cars I've bought as a result of making *Cars That Rock*. First there was the Richard Petty Mustang, then the Jaguar Project 7, and then the racing Mini – but we'll get to them later! I never realized this telly business could be so darned expensive.

5 JAGUAR

TEST DRIVING WHERE VULCAN BOMBERS USED TO TAKE OFF

> ❝ **We lurch around the track like a drunken snake – until the inevitable happens.** ❞

I f you're a fan of AC/DC, you'll know that we do a song called 'Big Balls' and that the chorus goes like this:

"Some balls are held for charity
And some for fancy dress
But the biggest balls I've ever seen
Belong to Jaguar legend Norman Dewis."

Well, alright, I've changed the words a little bit (sorry, Angus). Fact is that I am in total awe of 94-year-old Norman. He is the man who, as chief test engineer for Jaguar, helped develop every one of their models from the mid-1950s onwards. He still has the energy of a man half his age, and he loves to flirt with pretty women. They just don't make people like Norman any more.

Norman's career spanned the glory years of Jaguar, which meant he worked with company founder William Lyons, who started out making motorcycle sidecars in a Blackpool side street and ended up the boss of one of the greatest car companies in the world. Lyons had an unerring eye for beautiful design. He was also a businessman who was always looking to cut costs. "He was a tight old bugger," says Norman.

Lyons' penny-pinching meant that his cars flew out of the showrooms, however. The Jaguar E-Type is regularly named as Britain's favourite car – its sheer beauty caused Enzo Ferrari a few sleepless nights – and yet when it was launched in 1961 it sold for just over £2,000. No-one could believe how Jaguar did it at that price.

To many car enthusiasts, the E-Type is still Jaguar's greatest-ever

ABOVE A classic Jaguar E-Type – what else is there to say?

OPPOSITE ABOVE The command centre of the famous E-Type.

OPPOSITE BELOW Simply the greatest car to look at. It's just hard to believe this car was designed and built by regular English blokes.

car. I owned one myself for ages: a 1974 V12 roadster in silver with red interior, and it was absolutely gorgeous. If anything, it was a bit too gorgeous; the previous owner had chromed most of the engine bay and I was marked down for that when I entered it into a local classic car show for a bit of fun.

Lovely though it was, the V12 roadster can't compare with an early fixed-head coupé for looks – and I'm a sucker for coupés. I was very privileged indeed to get behind the wheel of the first E-Type, the actual car shown at the Geneva Motor Show in 1961, which is a fixed-head coupé finished in metallic grey. It was found by Jaguar historian Philip Porter as a rusting heap in 1976, but it wasn't until a quarter-of-a-century later that he could afford to get it restored.

I know it's a rude question, but bugger it, I have to ask: how much did it cost to restore? "One pound," replies Philip. "But that was because I cut a deal with the owner of a specialist Jaguar restoration business. He did a fantastic ground-up restoration of my car for a pound, and in return I gave him another E-Type that I owned, which was the first right-hand-drive car ever made. This car, 9,600 HP, was originally left-hand drive but was converted by Jaguar to right-hand drive after the Geneva Show."

It's also the car that famously achieved 150mph in *Autocar*'s road test back in 1961. Now, anyone who's owned an E-Type will know that even a brand-new one would struggle to top 140mph – so how did *Autocar* manage to achieve the magic 150mph?

"They prepared the engine very carefully,' says Philip, 'and made a few other little tweaks such as removing the front bumper overriders, which themselves accounted for a couple of mph. At the end of their test, the *Autocar* journalists finally squeezed 150.1mph out of this apparently standard E-Type."

Whatever its true top speed, an early E-Type is still a thing of joy to drive. It sounds glorious, it looks gorgeous, and it rides and handles incredibly thanks to Jaguar's pioneering independent rear suspension. For once, even though this car is over 50 years old, there's no need to make excuses. Its 0–60mph time is around seven seconds and it makes the most fabulous, aristocratic straight-six snarl getting there.

I like the E-Type coupé very much indeed, as you can probably tell. Even so, I've always had more of a hankering for the Mk2 saloon that was its counterpart in the 1960s. To me, its lines are just as perfect as anything produced by the finest French or Italian coachbuilders of the 1930s – and they're worth gazillions, whereas you can still pick up a decent Mk2 for £15–20,000. A 3.8-litre Mk2 is still the sexiest saloon car on the planet.

It's fast, too, which is why they were a favourite with '60s bank robbers. Great Train Robber Bruce Reynolds once said that when he was looking for a getaway car to steal in London, he'd try to find a Mk2 Jag with a British Racing Drivers' Club badge on the front, because the engine would probably have been tuned up a bit.

The engine that Bruce revered, and which powered all these classic Jags from the day the XK120 sports car was launched in 1948, was a superb straight-six with twin overhead camshafts. It was reliable and it provided scorching performance. Amazingly, it stayed in production until 1992 – a whole 44 years – and it even found its way into the Scorpion light tank. With the Jag engine installed, the eight-tonne Scorpion could reach 50mph.

It was this engine that gave Jaguar a string of motorsport victories during the 1950s, including five outright wins at Le Mans. And the man who saw it all happen was Norman Dewis, who joined Jaguar in 1952. He navigated Stirling Moss in a C-Type on the Mille Miglia, raced a D-Type at Le Mans – yet all this was part of Norman's everyday work as the chief development engineer, putting more than a million miles on cars to suss out their weak points and suggest ways to fix them.

When I met Norman at Jaguar's heritage workshop, I took an immediate liking to the man – how can you not admire someone who wears cowboy boots and a bootlace tie at the age of 94? He has a wonderful sense of humour and a fantastic memory, not least of the many record-breaking runs he did for Jaguar during the mid-50s.

One of these involved him being shoehorned into a standard XK120 roadster with an all-enclosing Perspex bubble instead of a windscreen, to improve the aerodynamics. It worked – Norman

coaxed this otherwise unmodified sports car up to 172.4mph – but the lack of air inside the sealed cockpit almost caused Norman to pass out. He remembers: "When the mechanic finally opened the canopy, I gave a big gasp. He looked surprised and said, 'Your face is like a big red tomato!'"

I bet he will have been remembering that canopy a lot more fondly when I almost gave the poor guy pneumonia, taking him for a ride in a D-Type at Jaguar's testing facility in Warwickshire. This place used to be an airbase for nuclear V-bombers, so it has an incredibly long main straight. Believe me, you need it when you're at the wheel of a D-Type. This thing was built to run at Le Mans; it can do 170mph. The day scheduled for our filming is cold and wet. Not ideal for driving a D-Type at speed. Especially one valued at £10 million.

For the driver, it's like being in a jet fighter from the early '50s. You sit low in the cockpit, surrounded by flat, black-painted sheets of alloy housing military-style dials and switches. Press the starter button and the D-Type's straight-six erupts into life, brap-brapping through the side-exit exhaust. Pull the gear lever back into second before pushing it into first, to ease the non-synchromesh gearchange. Then – floor it.

I've driven a C-Type on the Mille Miglia, and that felt seriously fast, but the D-Type takes the adrenaline to a whole new level. It's a much lighter car than you'd expect, weighing just 870kg, so the wonderful Jaguar engine doesn't have to work terribly hard to get the car flying. It just pulls and pulls, the rev-counter needle sweeping around the big Smiths dial, never seeming to run out of breath.

Unlike poor old Norman, who is fully exposed to the ice-cold blast of the slipstream because there's no windscreen on the passenger's side. Before our run, the TV director had instructed me to ask

OPPOSITE, ABOVE The C-type that Mark Dixon and I drove in the Mille Miglia in Brescia.

RIGHT Waiting with Norman for the film crew (again) in the D-type in the cold. What a good sport he was – there's no leg room where he sits.

OPPOSITE BELOW A white Jaguar XK120 Roadster.

BELOW ... the film crew arrive. And we alert the media!

Norman some questions as we're driving along, but you can't hear a wretched thing over the wind noise and I suspect we're both deaf as a post anyway. I can see Norman nodding in response to my questions, but I think he's just watching my lips move…

But he's a tough old bird. Just how tough is brought home to me when I mention that I did the Mille Miglia over four days in 2014. "Four days?" exclaims Norman incredulously. "In 1952 I did it with Stirling Moss in 11 hours!" And he's absolutely right. Norman and Stirling drove all but 100 miles of the 1,000-mile race – they crashed out near the end – in 11 hours, 29 minutes and 58 seconds. Like I said, they don't make 'em like that any more.

During the Mille Miglia I got to know Jaguar's head of design, Ian Callum, who is also a total car nut. When he was a child, he sent some of his drawings to Jaguar, explaining how he wanted to be a car designer. Blow me if Jaguar's vice chairman William "Bill" Heynes didn't write him a long letter back with some pointers on how to go about it. It was Bill Heynes who had developed Jaguar's XK engine back in the 1940s, so he was a very big cheese indeed in the Jaguar world.

Amazingly, Ian went on to realize his dream, and he's the man responsible for the current crop of Jaguars, from the big XJ saloon to the recent F-Type sports car. I suggest to Ian that designing a car is maybe a bit like writing a song, and he agrees. "You come up with an idea – and it might be quite random – and then you've got to refine it and refine it, while not losing sight of that initial spontaneity," he explains.

Ian adds that he would love to be a songwriter; I don't tell him that I also wanted to be a car designer when I was a kid, and that I still have my school exercise book sketches for the Brian Johnson Special, surely one of the greatest cars that never was, and a tragic loss to the British motor industry.

The F-Type is a fantastic sports car, a truly worthy successor to the E-Type. There are several different versions and they're all quick, even the entry-level V6 model, but the top-spec V8 is a real road-burner. It puts 542bhp out through the rear wheels and, let me tell you, even the traction control systems struggle to keep that amount of power in check. It's my kinda car.

Oddly, though, the F-Type roadster didn't do a lot for me when I first sat in one, at a racetrack in France. But now they've brought out a new model based on the F-Type. It's called the Project 7, and they're only making 250 of them

The Project 7 is 80kg lighter than an F-Type roadster, but its V8 has been hotted up to 567bhp, which is 25bhp more powerful than the F-Type R's. The suspension is firmed up front and rear, and there's a whole armoury of splitters and diffusers, plus a ruddy great wing on the back, to increase downforce and keep it glued to the tarmac.

BELOW and RIGHT The Scots have given us much to be thankful for – Robbie Burns, Billy Connolly, smoked salmon, sporrans, Irn Bru, haggis, *The White Heather Club*, Hamilton Academicals – and now the impressive Jaguar F-type, designed by a Scotsman, Ian Callum.

LEFT The shapely rear of the Jaguar Project 7. Lovely bum.

BELOW Mike Cross, Jaguar's chief engineer, and I discuss the Project 7. He was actually saying, "If you bend it, you mend it."

OPPOSITE I try my hand at "drifting".

With all that power – and no roof, because the Project 7 is very much a speedster and doesn't have a proper soft-top – it will be ideal for track days, where lucky owners can play at being the Earl of Oversteer to their hearts' content. Figuring I needed a bit of practice, I asked Jaguar's top test driver, Mike Cross, to give me a few pointers.

Mike is a very unassuming kind of bloke who looks as though he should be presenting the weather on TV. But get him behind the wheel of a fast car and he turns into a speed demon, the King of the Four-Wheel Drift. Mike has been responsible for developing the F-Type since it was just a gleam in Ian Callum's eye.

Slip into the tombstone-shape quilted leather seats, buckle up the four-point harness, press the starter button and the 5-litre supercharged V8 awakes with a sharp bark, crackling and popping on the overrun. It sounds as raw as an uncooked steak, and just as meaty. Trickle out onto the test track and gather some speed, ready for the long straight where Vulcan bombers used to take off.

OK, time to give it some gas... *Whoooah!* This thing is fast. The whole experience is utterly intense: there's the roar of the V8 ripping out of the quad exhaust pipes, and the white noise of the slipstream whooshing over the open cockpit, and meanwhile the speed just keeps on rising, 130, 140, 150... If you have the bottle, Project 7 will keep going to an electronically limited 186mph. That's one hell of an adrenaline rush in a car without a roof.

Anyone can go fast in a straight line, however. Holding a car on opposite lock in a controlled slide, known as drifting, takes real skill.

It's not just about speed, it involves finesse. And now I'm going to see if I have what it takes.

With Mike in the passenger seat alongside me, we enter a big circle of track that's perfect for an endless drift. "Hold it in third gear, in Sport mode, and jab the throttle," instructs Mike, but try as I might I can't get the tail out and the car just wants to plough straight on. Then Mike turns the traction control off, and suddenly the back end gets a lot more lively as 567bhp tries to find its way onto the tarmac.

Hanging the back end out now isn't the problem; keeping it at just the right angle, using exactly the right combination of opposite-lock steering and throttle, is much trickier. We lurch around like a drunken snake until the inevitable happens – we spin through 180°.

Mike suggests moving up a gear, to get some more momentum. Bad idea. Within seconds I've lost it and I'm going off-piste onto the grass. On the TV show you can see the camera crew rushing over to check that we're alright. I even swear a couple of times, which of course is totally out of character.

You'd have to be a fanatical petrolhead to want one of these 250 very special Jaguars – which is why I put my order in straight away. But I won't be practising any drifting unless there's a hell of a big run-off area. What you don't see on the TV show is Mike driving me at full chat around the test track in the Project 7, running wide on a corner and taking out a whole load of signposts. I wasn't the only one who swore that time. The Project 7 is a real wolf in sheep's clothing, and I love it.

6 | LAMBORGH

HINI

LAMBORGHINI

> ## " Ferrari had the prancing horse, but my father wanted something with the bigger balls. "

My mother was Italian, which explains why I feel such an affinity for Italy – and especially for its cars. My mum and dad met during the war, when she was living in her native Frascati and he was one of the Allied soldiers chasing out the Germans; she gave everything up to marry my dad and come and live in the cold and rainy north-east. That's true love for you.

Although most of her family disapproved of the match, her sisters supported her and they used to send us parcels of secondhand clothes. Wrapped up among the clothes would be bundles of the Italian newspaper *Oggi*, and in one of those papers there was a report on the Mille Miglia road race. I couldn't speak a word of Italian, of course – I was only about seven – but I loved the fabulous pictures of Ferraris and Maseratis and Alfa Romeos blasting along those Italian country roads. When I asked my mum what they were doing, she told me: "That is the Mille Miglia – the greatest race in the whole world!"

In 2014 I achieved my life-long ambition to compete in the modern revival of the Mille Miglia, driving a 1953 C-Type Jaguar, and it was fantastic. I recognized some of the locations we were passing through – hurtling through, would be more accurate – from the trip I'd made a few months earlier to visit Lamborghini. Sadly, you will never see a Lamborghini on the Mille Miglia, because it's only open to cars that competed on the original event. The last of the "proper" Milles took place in 1957, and the first Lamborghini appeared in 1964.

Like nearly all the car companies we've featured in *Cars That Rock*, Lamborghini owed its existence to the bloody-minded determination of one man. He was called Ferruccio Lamborghini, and he grew up in the Italian countryside among a family of grape farmers. During

ABOVE This is what the Lamborghini legend began with. I think he got stuck behind too many, and decided to make something faster.

OPPOSITE ABOVE Tonino and I chat at the Lamborghini Museum near Bologna.

OPPOSITE BELOW I sit in Ferruccio's first racing car – a Fiat Topolino! It honestly looks like a big kids' toy car.

LEFT I read the menu, while Tonino pretends he can't find any money in his pocket.

BELOW and **OPPOSITE** Ferruccio's very own Lamborghini Miura – pulled out of the museum so we could give it a drive. But they forgot to put petrol in it.

the Second World War he served as a mechanic with the Italian Army, where he is said to have made himself indispensible by burning all the workshop manuals – which, being a natural mechanic, he didn't need.

After the war, as Italy struggled to get back on its feet, Ferruccio realized that there would be a good market for a low-cost tractor and started a business making them. (It's strange how often tractors and supercars are linked. The owner of Aston Martin, David Brown, whose initials are on all the "DB" Astons like James Bond's DB5, also started out making tractors, and Ferdinand Porsche was designing tractors back in the 1930s, well before he got into making sports cars.)

Ferruccio did so well from the tractor business that within a decade or so he was able to buy his first Ferrari. But the experience wasn't a happy one.

"The clutch kept breaking in his Ferrari," I was told by Ferruccio's nephew Fabio during my visit to the Lamborghini museum. "My uncle worked out that it was too small to cope with the power of the engine, and so he put in a clutch from one of this tractors, which worked fine.

"Ferruccio then went to see Mr Ferrari, and said, 'Look, I can supply you with this clutch, which is cheaper than the one you're using and won't break.' But Enzo Ferrari wasn't interested. 'Go back to driving your tractors,' he said."

So Ferruccio decided he was going to build his own supercar, one

that would be better than any Ferrari. It was called the Lamborghini 350GT, and it went into production in 1964, with a front-mounted V12 engine. It looked incredibly sleek and futuristic, and when one influential American journalist road tested the 350GT, he headed his story: "This one will give Ferrari a migraine".

When I visited the Lamborghini museum, I was shown around by Ferruccio's son Tonino, whose English is only slightly better than my Italian. But he speaks enough to tell me why Ferruccio chose the symbol of a fighting bull for the Lamborghini badge. "Ferrari had the prancing horse, but my father wanted something more aggressive – something with the bigger balls!" he explained, making suggestive gestures with his cupped hands. Some things are universal in any language.

All the iconic Lamborghinis are on display in the museum, but the one that will always catch your eye is a bright red Countach, the car that adorned a million posters in a million teenage boys' bedrooms during the 1980s. The name is impossible to translate, but it's basically an exclamation in the local dialect – when people first saw the new car they would go, "Cor, what a Countach!". I'm not making that up; it's absolutely true.

Incredibly, this wedge-shaped cruise missile was first shown in 1971, complete with lift-up "scissor" doors. Even though it was launched at the worst possible time, when Italy was crippled by anti-capitalist

demonstrations, stringent tax laws, fuel shortages and new speed limits, it was a success because it just looked so outrageous. There's a story of how a Lamborghini test driver once parked an early Countach in a field, so he could re-cquaint himself with a former girlfriend he'd just spotted walking along the side of the road. The farmer whose field it was saw the car and came storming over to deal with the trespasser – but when the door hissed upwards and the driver stood up, he turned white as a sheet and rushed back to his tractor, convinced that aliens had landed in the Italian countryside.

But my love affair with Lamborghini began a few years before the Countach. If you've ever seen *The Italian Job* – the original, with Michael Caine and Benny Hill and Noel Coward, not the awful remake with Mark Wahlberg – then you'll recognize the Lamborghini Miura, which is being driven in the opening sequence by the cool dude wearing the shades, to the soundtrack of Matt Monro crooning 'On Days Like These'. About 30 seconds later he has an unfortunate coming together with a bulldozer that someone has carelessly parked in a tunnel.

The Miura is the car that came before the Countach. It was introduced in 1966 and is often called the world's first supercar, as well as being one of the most beautiful designs ever created. But the one

that Tonino is ushering me towards outside the museum is a rather special example. "This was my father's personal car," he announces as we come up behind a blood-orange Miura.

Riding in Ferruccio's very own Miura should have been one of the most memorable experiences of my life. And in a way, it was. We both get into the car – Tonino in the driver's seat, me alongside – and I realize then why they remove the testicles from sardines before they put them in those little tins. There's hardly any room. And it's hot. And then Tonino turns the ignition key, and it goes "Rurr-rurr-rurr" and nothing happens. The battery's flat. And there's no petrol in it.

Now, they've known for two months we were coming today – but this is Italy. Someone goes off to find a fuel can, and eventually we get the car started, and head off down the road towards the farm where Ferruccio spent his childhood, and where they've recreated the little workshop he had in one of the sheds.

We reach the beginning of the estate, where there are gates and a long dirt track winding up to the farm. The car gets halfway up it, and… dies. So we walk the rest of the way, which takes forever because it seems like miles, me desperately trying to think of something to say to Tonino when neither of us speaks the other person's language. But

OPPOSITE I get into leather.

OPPOSITE BELOW LEFT A seamstress in the Lamborghini factory – and her great work.

OPPOSITE BELOW RIGHT And look what she made for me...

RIGHT I say, "I swear, it's this long". Ranieri Niccoli looks sceptical.

BELOW Ranieri Niccoli gives me the factory tour in Santa Agata Bolognese.

the wonderful thing about Italians is that they never get embarrassed when things go wrong, because their whole lives are spent like that – it's why they've had about 65 different governments. You just have to go with the flow.

One thing you can't fault Italians for, though, is their enthusiasm. They are the most passionate nation on earth, as I found out when I met a father-and-son team who'd put a Lamborghini V12 engine into... a Fiat 500. And not the modern, big 500 that's the size of a Mk1 Transit van, but the original 1950s model.

In doing this, Gianfranco and Leonardo were only doing what Ferruccio himself had done back in the 1940s, when he took a Fiat Topolino – the 500's predecessor, with even less power – threw away the body and tweaked the engine until it would do 100mph. He entered the 1948 Mille Miglia but crashed out after 700 miles, and that was the end of Ferruccio's competition career.

Gianfranco and Leonardo play around with Fiat 500s, and the Lamborghini-engined 500 is the third in a series that began with one of them challenging the other to put a Porsche flat-six in a 500, which was followed by a return match involving a Ferrari V8 and a 500, and ended with them both being bet by journalists that they couldn't shoehorn a Lamborghini V12 into a 500. They managed it, although they had to throw away the Fiat chassis and make a new one out of box-section steel, and then widen the original Fiat body massively.

The engine is a 6.2-litre V12 from a first-generation Murciélago, and it takes up most of the interior – you're basically sitting in an engine bay. But the attention to detail is fantastic, from the rev-counter mounted in the middle of the steering wheel, to the "500" badging that's been modified to read 588CV – which is the Continental way of saying this car has 580 horsepower.

Bear that figure in mind, while I tell you how we go to a local go-kart

ABOVE LEFT Modified Fiat 500s with various supercar engines in them, in the garage near Viterbo. These two boys are bloody incredible innovators.

ABOVE RIGHT Father and son, Gianfranco and Leonardo, show me the impossible challenge they have taken a wager to complete.

LEFT They did it – a Lamborghini Murcielago V12 engine in a humble Fiat 500. This is David Copperfield stuff.

OPPOSITE We take this strange mutation of a machine out for a nocturnal prowl. There are no seatbelts, very Italian.

track. For action filming of the Fiat-Lamborghini love child at night, and Giancarlo offers to drive me round the circuit. When I ask him whether there are any seatbelts, he laughs in that typically Italian way, before adding that he is "not a good pilota..." He wasn't kidding, either, although in the TV footage it looks as though we're doing about 40mph when it felt a hell of a lot faster. You can hear me start to sing as I'm being driven round the track, some Italian pop song from the 1950s that my mother used to sing to me when I was little. It's a habit I've always had when I'm scared, as if by singing I can ward off anything bad that's going to happen to me.

Which reminds me ... someone asked me recently whether being in front of a big engine like a Lamborghini V12 and racing around a circuit is like standing in front of the band when I'm doing an AC/DC gig, with all that power and noise behind me, and the adrenaline coursing through my body. It's a good question. AC/DC is one of the loudest bands on the planet, and it's a form of engine that's pumping out music when it's firing on all cylinders. Thank God that these days we have "in-ears" – tiny microphones to relay what you're singing – because when I started out I couldn't hear a damn thing and I had to rely on muscle memory, which I didn't enjoy at all.

Ironically, after all those decades being on stage, it was a race car that made me deaf in my left ear. I was at Watkins Glen circuit in the USA, racing a 1600cc Royale "screamer", and I forgot to put my ear plugs in, so when I was about 40 minutes through the hour-long race my ear suddenly went "pouf!" and started pouring out blood, and that was that. I never had a problem when I was belting out rock 'n' roll.

But back to Italy, and to another famous race circuit. When I visited Lamborghini, the guys had lined up a surprise trip to Imola, where they wanted to show me their latest Gallardo Super Trofeo race car. I thought I was just going to sit in it, but no, this is Italy...

The Gallardo has been a massive success for Lamborghini, in production for more than 10 years and racking up as many sales as all the other models of Lamborghini put together. Think about that for a moment: half of all the Lamborghinis ever sold are Gallardos. And here's something else to think about: when Audi (which has owned Lamborghini since 1998) wanted to produce its own supercar, the R8, it based it on the Gallardo.

Without a race heritage like Ferraris, but with lots of cash-rich customers buying Gallardos like they were going out of fashion, Lamborghini decided in 2009 to set up its own one-marque race series, in which different teams all drive specially tuned Gallardos. It's called Super Trofeo and it's one of the fastest single-make series in the world, with top speeds north of 200mph.

That's a sobering thought at a circuit like Imola, which was the scene of one of the worst weekends in modern Grand Prix history. In three separate incidents during the 1994 San Marino Grand Prix, Rubens Barichello was injured, and Roland Ratzenberger and Ayrton Senna – one of the greatest drivers of all time – died. And now here I am, 20 years later, about to drive a circuit I don't know in a 200mph racing Lamborghini.

For the Super Trofeo series, the Gallardo has been given an aerodynamic makeover to make it stick to the track instead of taking off into space (where it surely belongs), and inside it's as stark and functional as a laboratory. All I can see is a dashtop the size of a football field, and directly in front of me a VDU which will scroll down all kinds of important information, while the naked steering column holds a pair of flappy paddles like the wings of a starfighter in *Star Wars*.

Foot on the brake, flick the kill-switch on, press the starter button and – *vroom!* The 570bhp V10 gets your nipples hard in a way that even Sophia Loren might struggle to match. Moving out of the pit lane, the blare of the exhaust transforms from a snarl to a bloodcurdling howl as the revs rise, and suddenly we're travelling fast and I'm really having to concentrate hard, feeling my way around a circuit I've never driven before at speeds of up to 170mph.

Into a chicane, flick the left-hand paddle once, twice, and the engine roars like an angry T-Rex and I'm on the brakes, but it's tighter than I was expecting and the car runs wide – boy, this thing is twitchy! It's a crazy machine, a total adrenaline fix, with a stupefying amount of power. It's bloody fantastic.

But the maddest thing of all is that Lamborghini has let me loose in its brand new race car, wearing jeans and a borrowed helmet, on one of the trickiest circuits I've ever driven. No questions about my previous experience, no awkward discussions about insurance, just go out and enjoy yourself. That's why I love Italy.

OPPOSITE A Lamborghini Aventador Roadster LP700-4 in a garage at Imola. Jeez, it's beautiful.

RIGHT Mario Fasanetto, Lamborghini's racing team driver, lets me near their new Gallardo Squadra Corse. What an intimidating track. I change my name to "Testicoli di Toro".

BELOW Incredibly – and very generously – Lamborghini let me drive it around Imola!

OPPOSITE MIDDLE A dull box.

OPPOSITE, ABOVE LEFT Me, up close and personal with a Lamborghini Aventador V12. I must admit I got a bit of a stiffy.

OPPOSITE BELOW A machinist disappears inside an engine. We never saw him again.

OPPOSITE, ABOVE RIGHT Ranieri shows me how big his is...

RIGHT ... and other scenes from the factory floor.

ABOVE Ranieri shows me the Lamborghini production line.

LAND ROVE

CONFESSIONS OF AN OFF-ROAD VIRGIN

ER

LAND ROVER

I never understood the appeal of Land Rovers – ever since I was a kid, I've wanted to go fast, not slow. My brother Maurice is the Land Rover fan. He has two of them, a 1968 Series 2A model and a new Defender. He runs a music festival catering business called Gig-a-bite (see what he did there?) and it is not unknown for festival sites to get just a little bit muddy, so his Defender comes in handy for pulling trailers in and out of fields.

The reason I never "got" Land Rovers is because I'd never been off-roading. Not proper off-roading, anyway. Back in the early '80s I had a big Chevy Blazer that I used for rabbit shooting with the local Northumbrian hill farmers. They didn't know what to make of it – "It's all covered in chroo-mium!" – and, of course, they had ratty old Land Rovers that were like sheds on four wheels. If it rained, you stayed drier if you stood outside.

The Chevy worked just fine on grassy moorland, but I never took it anywhere like as challenging as the estate at Eastnor Castle in Herefordshire, which Land Rover has used to test and demonstrate its vehicles for more half a century. On the 5,000-acre estate there are off-road tracks that would stop a tank. It's the perfect place to find out what a Land Rover can do.

The man who knows how to do it better than anyone else is Roger Crathorne, who joined the company in 1963 and has only just retired after a lifetime of testing Land Rovers to the limit off-road. He really is known as "Mr Land Rover". And Roger pulled the short straw of

BELOW With Roger Crathorne – aka Mr Land Rover – the world's foremost Land Rover expert.

OPPOSITE ABOVE Huey – one of the first Land Rovers ever built – comes through the gate towers of Eastnor Castle.

OPPOSITE BELOW Me at Huey's wheel. Huey rattled a great deal, and I swear I lost a testicle.

> " If I could only have one vehicle for the rest of my life? A long-wheelbase Defender. "

sitting beside me when I had my first drive of an old Landy. First, though, he explained how it came about.

"Just after the Second World War, Rover's technical director Maurice Wilks bought an army-surplus Jeep for his family to drive when they were at their holiday cottage on Anglesey, off the North Wales coast," he told me. "They were playing around with it on the beach one day in the spring of 1947, and his brother Spencer – who was the MD of Rover – suggested that Rover should build something like the Jeep, only better. The story goes that they drew an outline on the sand of what it might look like, and that became the Land Rover."

I love that story, the idea of these two middle-aged blokes drawing a big picture in the sand with a stick. But you can easily imagine how it might have happened, because the Land Rover is all straight lines, with hardly a curve in it. It's purely functional, and that's why it lasted so long. It transcended the whims of fashion.

The Land Rover that I got to drive with Roger is not just any old Landy – it is the oldest Land Rover, the very first one to roll out of the factory in March 1948. What made it different from anything else on the market was its permanent four-wheel drive system, with a second gearbox that gave you a choice of driving in "high range" – for road use – or "low range", for off-roading.

Mind you, with a top speed even in high range of only 50mph, you don't need to use 'low' unless you're really in the sticky stuff. The original Land Rover is incredibly, well, agricultural. You sit hunched upright over a huge steering wheel, stomping on pedals that are big enough to operate with Wellington boots, and you fish for a willowy gear lever that's topped with a knob like a flat pebble. First gear is a real stump-puller – literally so – so you change up quickly; the stiff suspension and short wheelbase make everything rattle and bang as we bumble down Eastnor's stoney tracks, and we've not been driving 30 seconds before the TV crew's cameras and microphones fall off.

But it's fantastic fun to drive. It's so short – at 11ft long, it's more than two feet shorter than a new Vauxhall Corsa! – you can throw it about like a rally car, and its willing little 1600cc engine gives it the enthusiasm of an eager puppy. The idea was that you could use this vehicle on the farm – or the game reserve if you were somewhere in the Colonies – and then take the little woman into town for a night out. People were hardier in those days.

It was an incredible success. Partly that was sheer luck: a shortage of steel after the Second World War meant that the Land Rover body

was made from aluminium, and therefore it couldn't rust. But mostly it was because it was just what the world needed as it struggled to get back on its feet after the war. They say that a Land Rover was the first vehicle to be seen by an estimated one-third of the world's population, because it could go places that nothing else had been able to reach.

The British Army was quick to realize they were onto a good thing here, and they ordered thousands and thousands of Land Rovers from the early 1950s onwards. That's why so many Land Rovers are painted dark green: the early ones were finished in a tasteful light green, but Land Rover changed the standard colour when the big military contracts started coming in. And it was the Army – plus dozens of other armed forces across the world – who really pushed the development of the Landy to its limits.

One of the more bizarre experiments was an amphibious Land Rover. There have been various attempts made over the years, and I got to try one that was built in 1982 with the idea of carrying troops over large expanses of water. So they took me out onto a lake...

Now, I'm not good with anything involving rudders and propellors, and my first sight of the amphibious Landy was not a reassuring one. It looks like a regular Land Rover with a load of oil drums welded to the outside. But I love the way that the front indicators have red and green lenses in them – for Port and Starboard, of course. Someone at Land Rover clearly had a sense of humour.

The scariest bit is driving off the land and into the water. Then you move a lever to engage the propellor and you use another lever to waggle the rudder. Once you're in, it's not the fastest thing on water, but to borrow a line from the great Dr Johnson – no relation – it's not how well it's done, it's the fact that you're actually sailing in a Land Rover that's the killer. At least, I think he said something like that.

In theory, the amphibious Landy could be made ready to take to the waves in about 10 minutes, but that's 10 minutes too long when you

OPPOSITE An amphibious Land Rover.

LEFT Martin Brown from the Motor Heritage Museum at Gaydon welcomes me aboard. It felt weird, seeing a tiller next to the gear stick.

BELOW LEFT We prepare to go to sea.

BELOW RIGHT The Land Rover sails away, with Captain Johnson on board, shivering his timbers. We were passed by two ducks and a trout.

have a bunch of Cold War Soviets chasing your arse, and the Army politely said, "No thanks, old boy" when asked if they'd like to buy a few.

The standard Land Rover was so good, however, right from the start, that the basic shape and formula hasn't changed in 67 years. Obviously, the engines and gearboxes have been updated, but the only significant difference between a 1948 Landy and one made in 2015 is that the old one has leaf springs and the new one has coils – a change introduced back in the early '80s to improve off-road ability by allowing the axles to move up and down more. There's still a hefty chassis made out of box-section steel, and the vehicles are still assembled by hand – as I saw for myself when I visited the Land Rover factory at Solihull.

In 2015, they're producing nearly 500 Land Rovers a week here. Actually, they're not called Land Rovers any more: the marketing men would rather you call them Defenders, which is a brand name just like Discovery or Range Rover. This year will be a bumper one

for Land Rover – sorry, Defender – sales, because at the end of 2015 production will cease forever in Europe. Blame the bureaucrats in Brussels and their fondness for Elf and Safety; the Defender is just too old-fashioned to meet their new regulations. It looks likely that India or China may buy up the old production line, however – they know a good thing when they see it.

Some poor sod will have recently taken delivery of a Defender with a windscreen fitted by yours truly. Not a lot of people know that before I was in the band, I used to fit car windscreens for a living. That was back in the '70s, so of course the procedure is identical for a 2015 Defender. They still use a bit of string tucked inside the screen rubber to pull it into position. You won't see that in any other car factory today.

Already I'd fallen for the Defender's character, and I hadn't even taken one off-road yet. To rectify that situation, a very experienced off-roader called Mark "Frosty" Frost put me in the hot seat of a new

LEFT I go down memory lane and fit a windscreen at the Land Rover factory in Solihull.

BELOW I am the first person to ever drive this Defender – a few yards off the production line. I still find it odd that they're discontinuing this vehicle. It just looks right.

OPPOSITE CLOCKWISE FROM TOP A soon-to-be-discontinued new Defender; the factory floor; robot riveters at work – no works canteen for these boys; I operate a robotic riveter. I'm sorry if that sounds kinky.

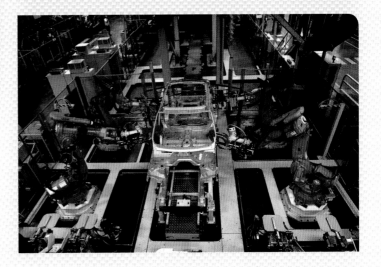

Defender 110 at Eastnor Castle's off-road course. Because I'm an off-road virgin, he broke me in gently. By getting me to drive along – not across – a river.

There's something incredibly exciting about driving through water that's deeper than a puddle. And there's a real technique to it, too. You have to go in slowly but then accelerate just enough to start a bow wave rolling in front of you, so that the depression behind it keeps water out of the air intake. Get it wrong, and water will enter the engine cylinders and lock everything solid. It doesn't compress nearly as well as air...

I soon realize that this whole off-roading business is a very technical exercise, just as demanding in its own way as racing or rallying. The biggest difference is that everything happens slowly. A lot of the skill comes in picking your route so that you don't beach the vehicle on a ridge – or slide into a tree. And the golden rule when coming down a steep slope is to keep both feet off all the pedals. Don't brake, because that could lock the wheels up and you'll start sliding out of control. Don't use any throttle; let the engine keep the speed under control by itself. And don't drive down at an angle, or you could end up tipping the vehicle over. It almost makes racing round a circuit look easy. At least most of that happens on the flat.

That's how you go off-roading. Unless, that is, you're taking part in an off-road race like the Dakar Rally. Then you throw everything I've just mentioned out of the window. This kind of off-roading is full-on, no holds barred and against the clock. It's physically exhausting – so imagine how difficult it must be when you're attempting it without the full complement of limbs that God gave you. The boys from Race2Recovery do just that.

Race2Recovery was the idea of two servicemen, Captain Tony Harris and Corporal Tom Neathway, who'd been blown up in Afghanistan. Tony had lost a leg below the knee; Tom had lost both legs and an arm. They set up Race2Recovery to show injured men like themselves just what is possible – and to let them experience the adrenaline rush that soldiering had once provided, and to do it as part of a team. "Rehabilitation focuses on the individual," explains Tony Harris. "Tom and I wanted to do something with common goals, so we could feel part of a team again."

When I catch up with the Race2Recovery team at a British cross-country rally in Dorset, two new team members are getting to grips with their first attempt at racing in a Land Rover Freelander. OK, it's the V6 version, but it's still basically the shopping car that yummy mummies use for the school run.

Grant White served for 23 years with the Royal Marines until he lost his right leg to a hit-and-run motorcyclist. This is his first off-road event – and it's about to be mine too. I'm to act as co-driver for a lap of the dusty, bumpy course, taking the seat normally occupied by Yanto

OPPOSITE Off-roading at Eastnor Castle estate in a Defender 110 (in and out of the American Dip). It was like diving off a cliff.

RIGHT Mark Frost, me and Rob Barr, my off road guides.

BELOW The 110 proves its worth. i really enjoyed the challenge. I fell in love with these trucks all over again.

JOY

ABOVE RIGHT and **LEFT** Race2Recovery driver Grant White driver and I get ready.

ABOVE MIDDLE Ben Gott, the Race2Recovery team boss shows me their Wildcat.

LEFT Strapped into the Wildcat – the car they hope to enter into the Dakar Rally.

OPPOSITE Standing between two great guys: driver Grant White (left) and co-driver Yanto Evans (right), both from Race2Recovery. These men make me proud, and privileged, to be in their company.

Evans, who had his leg shot to pieces in Iraq. Yanto tells me that my main task is to shout at Grant to slow down if he looks like breaking the car. As the old saying goes, to finish first, first you have to finish.

The course is laid out on a military training site, appropriately enough. Our Freelander is pretty stock apart from racing seats and harnesses, and a rollcage in case things go literally tits up. Grant guns the throttle and the Freelander leaps away; there's nothing for me to do except sit tight and give him lots of encouragement. Tell him to slow down? Bugger that! Go on, my son!

The Freelander is literally flying over bumps and crashing into dips as Grant gives it his all, but my "don't hold back" approach must be working because Grant crosses the finish line a whole minute sooner than he managed on his previous lap. Oops.

For me, though, this has been just a warm-up to the star turn: a flat-out lap in a proper Dakar rally weapon, all spaceframe chassis and thundering V8. Say hello to a Rambo Rover. Say hello to the Wildcat.

It looks vaguely like a Land Rover and the oily bits are all Land Rover, but that's as far as the relationship goes. Think of it more as a lightweight, superfast Hummvee, designed to cross horrendously difficult terrain at top speed. The beefy 4.6-litre Rover

V8 produces 283bhp and 292lb of torque – so it's no surprise to find that there's a massive 365-litre fuel tank amidships. "It costs £450 to fill up, if you feel like contributing some petrol money," teases driver and Race2Recovery founding member Ben Gott.

The Freelander felt quick, but the Wildcat goes like, well, like a scalded wildcat. I'm strapped into my seat so tight I can barely move and yet I feel like a loose sock in a washing machine – my arms and legs are flailing around like one of the Thunderbirds puppets as the Wildcat hurtles around the course. After two minutes I'm already knackered, and yet Dakar competitors have to endure it for up to 16 hours a day on flat-out stages that are hundreds of miles long.

Grant and Yanto have a difficult road ahead of them – both literally and metaphorically – but I sincerely hope that they achieve their goal of being the first pair of amputees to finish the Dakar.

Myself, I can't believe I've never been a Land Rover fan until now. Somebody asked me a question the other day: if I could have only one vehicle for the rest of my life, what would I choose? The answer is obvious: a long-wheelbase Defender. I used to think my brother Maurice was bonkers for being a Land Rover enthusiast. Now I think

8 | McLAREN

MIND-BOGGLING TECHNOLOGY IN THE CARS THAT GO UP TO ELEVEN

MCLAREN

Everyone has a story to tell about Ron Dennis, the feared and revered boss of McLaren who is infamous for his obsession with detail. One of my favourites is about the floor tiles in McLaren's HQ near Woking in Surrey. Supposedly, Ron refused to allow any tiles to be cut where they meet walls and doors – every room in the building had to be designed so that only whole floor tiles could be fitted.

Having been to the McLaren's Technology Centre – and it really is much more than just a factory where they build cars – I utterly believe that story. The building, which was designed by Norman Foster, is an amazingly futuristic design that's half buried underground. If you're a visitor, you park up outside an elevator shaft that whisks you down to seeming endless white corridors populated by beautiful women wearing white coats with pens and clipboards. It is just like being in a Bond film.

McLaren has been massively successful in Formula 1, with more than 180 Grand Prix wins, 12 Drivers' World Championships and eight Constructors' in its trophy cabinet. I try to follow Formula 1 wherever I am in the world and I'm a big fan of McLaren – although my heart really lies with Williams, because Frank Williams was born in South Shields and is a big-time Newcastle United supporter.

I went to the Technology Centre to find out more about McLaren's road cars, which are a relatively recent phenomenon and one that's aimed straight at the throat of Ferrari. McLaren's first supercar was the F1 of 1993, still held by many enthusiasts to be the purest, most thrilling car ever made. It had a mid-mounted 6-litre BMW V12 and the driver sat in the middle of the car, with passengers either side. Only

BELOW I approach the McLaren Starship, which appears to have landed in Woking.

OPPOSITE ABOVE The quietest, cleanest production line in the world.

OPPOSITE BELOW Kris Lawton and I walk past a modest £200,000-worth of McLaren 650S.

" **There's something about the P1 that's almost alien ... a living creature.** "

100 F1s were built and they're now worth millions of pounds each.

After the F1 there was a gap until the MP4-12C coupé came along in 2011, and the current version of that is called the 650S. They turn out seven of those a day, all handbuilt in a spookily silent assembly hall that is almost certainly cleaner than most hospital operating theatres. It's an obvious rival for the Ferrari 458, and it costs a similar amount of money.

The area that impressed me most as I was walking around was called the Geometric & Surface Validation department. Even the lettering over the door looked like something from *Space: 1999*. Inside, technicians sit in front of huge Apple Macs on white tubular desks, flanking a raised dais on which a McLaren chassis was being charted by a massive robot arm brandishing a ruby-tipped needle the size of a ballpoint pen refill. Every single car has to measure up; if there's the slightest discrepancy, it doesn't get any further.

When you see this kind of mind-boggling technology, the price tag for a 650S of about £200,000 starts to look quite reasonable. And if you're a Russian oligarch or an American internet billionaire, supercars like the 650S are two-a-penny. What you want is a hypercar: something, to quote my musical associate Nigel from Spinal Tap, that goes all the way up to 11.

What you want is a McLaren P1. Except that you can't have one: all of the 375 that are being built had sold out within six months. Even at the asking price of £866,000 each. That's how desirable a P1 is.

Fortunately, McLaren has kept one back as a demonstrator, and they are willing to let me loose in it. My instructor, Phil Quaife, looks young enough to be my grandson, and that's not helping my nerves. Normally, fast cars don't frighten me, but there's something about the P1 that's almost alien. Its body is a mass of organic curves, and from behind it's even more otherworldly, with sculpted LED tail-lights that seem to dissolve in and out of the rear haunches. It's like a living creature, a B-movie monster from Outer Space.

The technology inside this thing is otherworldly, too. The P1 is among the first of a new breed of hybrid supercars, where electricity is used to boost the horsepower provided by an internal-combustion engine. So, of the 903bhp available to a P1 driver, 727bhp is delivered by a twin-turbo, 3.8-litre V8, while the other 176bhp comes from an electric motor built into the drivetrain. This is Formula 1 stuff, using energy that would otherwise be lost under braking and deceleration to recharge the electric motor's batteries.

All that power obviously makes the P1 extremely fast. It's electronically limited to a top speed of 217mph, but if you took the speed restrictor off it would be good for about 255mph before aerodynamic drag won out. On a dark and dank day, on a narrow and twisty test track, 217mph seems plenty to be going on with.

Press the starter, and the twin-turbo V8 rumbles away to itself with a gruff, bassy exhaust note. Move out of the pit lane and onto the damp tarmac and it develops a character of its own, hard and race-edged. Start to build some confidence and it's an ever-present companion as you press on, constantly talking to you as the turbo does its stuff, muttering and hissing as you accelerate and brake. With its light steering and instant response, this car demands a high level of precision from its pilot; it rewards delicacy rather than brutality.

And yes, it is stunningly, jaw-droppingly fast. The electric motor helpfully fills in any gaps in the V8's torque delivery, bolstering the turbos as they spool up between gear changes. There's also a button you can press to give an instant surge of battery power, like engaging the afterburner on a jet engine. It's Dick Dastardly's Mean Machine out of *Wacky Racers*, brought to life.

OPPOSITE and **ABOVE**
McLaren's amazing P1 supercar.

Driving this car is a completely immersive experience. Of course, you can let the electronics do all the work and sort everything for you, but if you want optimum performance then you need the multi-tasking skills of a modern F1 driver. In that sense, it's a car for the computer-game generation. You don't just drive it and react to whatever the road throws up; you anticipate and programme and fiddle around with settings. Some people will love that sense of control. Me, I'm not so sure.

Let me give you an example of the downside to all this technology. For one of the TV shots, I was asked to walk into a hangar where the P1 was lurking moodily, fire it up and drive it out. Unfortunately, the gale-force wind blowing in through the hangar doors had convinced the P1 that it was already driving at high speed and had activated its aero settings – and they wouldn't allow the car to start. It took four engineers to rig up a workaround.

It's all a very long way from the car in which Bruce McLaren, who founded the company in 1963, cut his teeth. You can see Bruce's first car at the Technology Centre today, looking lost among the garish Can-Am and F1 machines: a humble 1929 Austin 7, with no wings or headlights and painted bright red. As a young teenager growing up in his native New Zealand, Bruce worked on it and won his first event in it when he was just 14.

As a child, Bruce had already overcome serious adversity.

Diagnosed with Perthes disease, which causes one hip joint to stop growing, he spent a couple of years confined to bed. After moving to England in 1959 to join the Cooper racing team, he promptly won his first Grand Prix at the age of 22. He won several more Grands Prix, and the Le Mans 24 Hours, before his tragic death while testing at Goodwood in 1970. He was not quite 33 years old.

McLaren is best known today for Formula 1, but Bruce's company diversified much more in the 1960s. In fact, its biggest success then was in the crazy world of Can-Am racing, one of the most outrageous race series there has ever been. Can-Am, which stood for Canadian-American, had no rules for maximum engine size or minimum weight. It ran for only nine seasons, 1966-74, and McLaren won two-thirds of the races it entered.

I own and race an example of the first Can-Am winner, which is a Lola T70. Much as I love it, I sometimes wish I'd bought a McLaren instead. There's just something about the McLaren; when you sit in it, you've a sense of entering unknown terroritory. They're not easy cars to drive.

Particularly not when you're at a short little circuit in England, where I got to try the McLaren M6B belonging to Anthony and Richard Taylor, father and son. It looks like a 1960s vision of a car from the future, finished in the bright orange colour that McLaren chose to set it apart from the traditional racing hues of red, green, blue and so on. "The earliest McLarens were black and silver, which are New Zealand's racing colours," explains Richard, "but Bruce decided those colours were too difficult to spot in a rear-view mirror!"

The McLaren M6B is from the early days of Can-Am, so it "only" has a 5.7-litre Chevy V8 developing around 600bhp – by 1974, Porsche's 917 was running a twin-turbo flat-12 that put out twice as much. But 600bhp is not to be sneezed at in a car weighing a little over 700kg. It's basically an engine wrapped in an eggshell.

Driver comfort comes very low down on the list of priorities. Just getting in is hard enough, especially when the car's owner has been

LEFT With Anthony and Richard Taylor, and a disassembled Mclaren M6B. Bruce Mclaren's masterpiece.

OPPOSITE The Mclaren M6B, 1968 model.

asked to sit alongside: poor Anthony has to squeeze his head the other side of a roll bar and crick his neck while I try to manhandle this monster around a circuit that feels like a go-kart track.

Bringing the Chevy V8 to life is like detonating a bomb: instantaneous and deafening. Pull away onto the track, and its percussive beat morphs into a raw growl as the revs rise. It is awesomely quick, but there's no way I can extract more than a hint of this car's performance on such a miniature circuit; I'm always on the brakes for the next corner, always having to be careful not to unleash too much power on the exit. The straights aren't long enough to give the V8 its head, the corners aren't fast enough to get some heat into the tyres.

Even so, I've had just a taste of what this car can do, and I'm smitten. Bruce and his fellow New Zealander Denny Hulme won so many races driving M6s in the 1967 Can-Am season that the series was nicknamed "the Bruce and Denny show".

Bruce died while testing the M6's successor, the M8, at Goodwood in 1970; some of the car's bodywork became detached, instantly destroying the aerodynamics that kept the car glued to the tarmac. Eerily, his death echoed something he'd written six years earlier about the fatal crash of team mate Timmy Mayer:

"Who is to say that he had not seen more, done more and learned more in his few years than many people do in a lifetime? To do something well is so worthwhile that to die trying to do it better cannot be foolhardy. It would be a waste of life to do nothing with one's ability, for I feel that life is measured in achievement, not in years alone."

The team picked itself up and carried on under the leadership of Bruce's business partner – and Timmy Mayer's brother – Teddy Mayer. With sponsorship from Marlboro, the now red-and-white McLarens took both the Drivers' and the Constructors' F1 World Championships in 1974, and another Drivers' title in '76.

McLaren's rollcall of F1 drivers is one of the most notable in race history. Fittipaldi and Hunt in the 1970s; Lauda, Prost and Senna

in the 1980s. Ron Dennis came onboard in 1981, merging his own race team with McLaren and soon assuming control of the combined outfit. Since Lewis Hamilton secured McLaren's most recent World Drivers' Championship in 2008, the ultimate prize has eluded them – but they are still the team to beat.

And that's the key word – "team". It doesn't matter how good your drivers are, if the tenths of a second they strive to shave off their lap times are wasted by a clumsy pit stop. The amount of effort that's devoted to achieving the fastest possible pit stop is unbelievable, as I found out during a training session inside the McLaren HQ.

There are 24 pit crew tasked with looking after a McLaren F1 car, and each of them has a single, very specific job to do. For a simple tyre change, three men are allocated to each wheel: one to take the wheel off, one to wield the air gun for the hub nut, and one to fit the new wheel and tyre. If they do it right, the whole operation from car stopping to car leaving should take barely two seconds.

When you're working at that kind of speed, there is literally no time to think about what you're doing; if you're doing that, you're too slow. It has to be instinctive. The McLaren boys spend as much time preparing mentally as they do physically, using techniques employed by Olympic athletes, while training to be fit as a butcher's dog.

These guys are like Wild West gun slingers, none more so than the bloke in charge of the air gun, which tightens and unlocks the wheel hubnuts at 150rpm. It's not an easy tool to control, and I

demonstrated that perfectly when they let me have a go: on my first attempt the gun slipped off the nut in a shower of expensive sparks, which added another 10 seconds to the tyre change. In a real race, that could have cost McLaren a win.

If there weren't so much at stake, this kind of obsession about saving fractions of a second would seem slightly mad – in the same way that the whole McLaren ethos of seeking perfection can appear unnecessarily over-the-top. The irony is that its cars are built by hand, and yet it's the humans who make this immaculate facility look slightly untidy. You can't help feeling that in Ron Dennis's perfect world, the only actual person working at McLaren would be the guy in the peaked cap who signs you in at the gate.

On the day we visited McLaren to film the TV show, we were scheduled to have an interview with the Ron Dennis himself. When we arrived, we were told that he couldn't make the appointment – something else had come up.

And you know what? I admire him for that. Chances are he had clients wanting to see him who were worth millions of pounds to his business, and that was a lot more important than giving some soundbites to an old rock 'n' roller making a TV programme. He has to get his priorities right.

McLaren is a modern British success story, and I think Bruce would be awestruck by what it's achieved and the quality of its engineering. Keep doing what you do, Ron (Ron).

OPPOSITE The Mclaren Formula One pit crew get a new recruit. Now this was nervy – these guys don't smile a lot.

RIGHT The new recruit gets kitted up.

BELOW It's pride of place for the McLaren F1 race car.

9 MG

AS ENGLISH AS A THATCHED COUNTRY PUB SERVING PINTS OF WARM BEER

MG

Silverstone at nine o'clock on Saturday morning: it's freezing cold and the track is damp. I'm strapped into a 420bhp MGB and I'm about to take it out for the first time. As I leave the pit lane to enter the track at all of 35mph, the back end slides out. I think: "*Whoa!* This is going to be interesting..."

I've been racing for 16 years and I'm not scared of powerful cars, but this MG frightens me. It's running slick tyres and I think we should swap to wets, but the owner doesn't think it's necessary. Within a single lap, everything goes horribly wrong. I'll tell you what happened in a minute.

MGs are not meant to be like this. They are friendly, cheery, happy little things. The man who invented them, Cecil Kimber, is a personal hero of mine. In 1921 he was working as a salesman for car company boss William Morris, who made plodding family saloons. Kimber thought there was money to be made by selling a sportier version at a higher price. So he took a humble "Bullnose" Morris and turned it into a handsome roadster. He called it an MG, because it was made at Morris Garages. Genius, eh?

Kimber's formula was a winner, and soon MG was established as a sub-brand of the Morris empire, with its own factory in Abingdon, just outside Oxford. From the late 1920s to the mid-50s, MGs were instantly identifiable by their handsome radiator grilles, flowing wings and distinctive octagonal MG badge. They weren't massively fast but they were fun – and I know, because I have one.

BELOW MG TC and I pose for the camera.

OPPOSITE ABOVE I drive John Day around Gaydon Motor Museum in "Old Number One". I wish I could have opened her up.

OPPOSITE BELOW "Old Number One" having a rest in the Museum garage.

> ## " I'm thoroughly enjoying myself ... until I notice Paul has turned slightly green. "

LEFT Two tasty vintage MGs...

BELOW ... and some more: Fred Body (MG car enthusiast and restorer) and I with two equally enjoyable sorts of "Old Speckled Hen". A man who enjoys keeping history alive, the backbone of the vintage car fraternity.

OPPOSITE Some say MG aren't half the cars they used to be ... but I don't agree.

I didn't set out to own it, mind. I never had an MG when I was growing up – I couldn't afford it. Where I lived, you only had an MG as a young man if you were going to college or your dad was a doctor. If he worked in a factory, forget it.

In recent years, though, I've been helping a good friend of mine to raise money for an Alzheimer's charity, which we dubbed Highway to Help. His name is Byron DeFoor and we sometimes race together. One day he asks if he and his wife can drop round the house for a few minutes. "Sure", I say, and they turn up at the door. There's this absolutely gorgeous MG TF parked outside. "Did you come in that?" I ask. "Naw, it's for you!" says Byron. "It's a thank you for all you've done for the charity."

This car is mint, in better condition than it would have left the factory, and I really didn't feel able to accept it. But Byron is richer than God, so in the end I said, "Thank you very much" and gave in gracefully. I love driving it, but there's no room for it in my garage in Florida, so most of the time it's on display in the Sarasota Classic Car Museum.

The MG TF was the last of the old-fashioned style MGs – and by 1954, when my car was made, it really was old fashioned. It could easily be mistaken for the MG roadsters that were made before the Second World War, and which became so popular with RAF pilots and American servicemen who were based in England during the war. It was these little MGs that helped kick-start the whole sports car scene in America afterwards, when the US Army and Airforce boys went home and took some of our MGs with them.

To the Americans, the MG was as English as a thatched country pub serving pints of warm beer – and there is actually a beer named after a famous MG. I got to drive it when I visited the MG Car Club's offices in Abingdon, which are on the site of the original factory. The beer is called Old Speckled Hen and it's now sold in more than 20 countries.

The car, though, was originally called Old Speckled 'Un. It was nicknamed this by the workers at Abingdon who used it as a factory hack before the war because of its unique fabric-covered body, which had flecks of silver mixed into the black material. MG called it a Featherweight Fabric Saloon but it wasn't a great

seller, and the original Old Speckled 'Un is the only one left.

MG enthusiast Fred Body spent three years trying to find this rare survivor, which had lain derelict in a garage for decades. It looked a wreck, but he rebuilt it from the chassis up in just 12 months. It's a charming old thing, and I particularly liked the headlight-dipping system: push a lever forward and a linkage turns the headlights so they're pointing downwards. Fan-tastic!

Powered by the Morris Cowley's 1800cc sidevalve engine, this early MG isn't the fastest thing on four wheels, but it's a pleasure to cruise along in, gear whine from the transmission almost drowning out the burble from the low-revving four-cylinder motor. The interior is a lovely place to spend time in, all red leather and light varnished woodwork, so who cares how long it takes to get to 60mph – or that you'll be going flat out when you get there?

Fred is typical of the modest yet hugely dedicated enthusiast that MGs attract, and always have done. Few of them, however, go to the

lengths that MG Midget owner Roy Locock has done. Quite literally. Since buying his 1977 Midget early in 2006, he has driven her all over the world. So far "Bridget the Midget" and Roy have visited 52 countries and travelled about 80,000 miles. And it all started with a packet of chewing gum.

"I'd always wanted a British sports car, and Bridget happened to be on display in the showroom when I popped into the garage to buy some gum," he told me. "I thought, if I don't buy it now, I never will. It wasn't until we reached Australia that I realized this was the most unreliable model that MG ever built."

Roy clearly has the sense of humour necessary for driving an old MG single-handedly around the world. I ask him whether he had much trouble on his trips. "Generally – yes," he deadpans. And he describes the Taliban mortar fire near his hotel in Pakistan as "nothing personal". Perhaps he was lucky, though. Bearing in mind that he was travelling through countries like Iran and Russia, a

ABOVE, LEFT and **OPPOSITE**
Four photos of the 1977 world-
travelling Bridget the Midget
– this car, like the Land Rover,
shows how British design after
the war was world-class. Mr
Locock is a classic eccentric
English car nut.

numberplate that begins with the letters "SPY" could have been a problem. "Fortunately, either they didn't notice or they enjoyed the joke," he says.

Roy's car was built towards the end of Midget production, which came in 1980, along with the closure of the MG factory. That was the end of MG sports cars until the early 1990s, when the success of Mazda's MX-5 had proved that there were still a lot of people who craved some wind-in-the-hair motoring. But they also wanted it in a modern car that was well built and handled sweetly, rather than some throwback to a bygone age.

The response from the Rover Group, which owned the MG name, was an all-new sports car in 1995 called the MGF. It was technically clever but it was let down by well-publicized problems with the head gasket that saw innumerable engines cooked. That was just one more woe to add to Rover Group's list of troubles in the late 1990s. They culminated in MG being sold off for a token £10 to a consortium

of managers and businessmen who wanted to keep this most British of marques alive at its base in Longbridge, Birmingham.

You have to hand it to the guys at Longbridge: they weren't giving up without a fight. If they saw an opportunity to sell some cars for minimal outlay, they'd go for it. Cecil Kimber would have been proud.

Unfortunately, they backed the wrong horse with one of the most bizarre MGs ever built. The MG XPower SV seemed to be the exact opposite of what MG had always stood for – cheap, simple fun. The SV was neither cheap nor simple. It was a super-coupé, with a carbon-fibre body and 320bhp Ford Mustang V8 engine. It looked striking and aggressive, but it wasn't pretty.

On paper, it made a kind of sense. The SV was actually a reworking of another car, the Mangusta, for which Rover had acquired the rights. The big advantage was that the Mangusta was already certified for sale in America. The big disadvantage was that carbon

fibre is a very difficult and expensive material for making cars out of.

The SV's carbon-fibre body had to be laid-up in Modena, Italy, and it's rumoured that each one cost £40,000. To build a whole car set Rover back £200,000 every time – and yet the retail price was £65,000. The SV no longer made any sense at all.

Nonetheless, Rover soon brought out a more powerful version, the SV-R, with a 385bhp version of the Mustang V8. But the example I was lucky enough to try out was the one-off 4.6-litre supercharged SV-S, which was in development when the project was finally killed off. This baby puts out about 450bhp and has been clocked at 185mph. Not bad for an MG.

You get some idea of the car's intentions from the full race harnesses draped over the quilted black leather seats. Slip them on, and let's go for a spin in the fastest production MG ever made.

Yee-ha! Jeez, this thing can shift! There's a great dollop of torque from that big American motor, and when you squeeze the throttle you can hear the supercharger whining above the bass-line bellow of the throbbing V8 as the scenery starts to blur past you at an exponentially increasing speed. This is supercar performance, alright, and it has the chassis to match. What it doesn't have, though, is the right badge on the bonnet.

There was a lot of hand-wringing when, after more twists and turns than a soap opera plot, MG was finally sold on to the Chinese company SAIC Motor in 2007. But, really, was that such a bad thing?

Thanks to the Chinese, MG is still producing cars at Longbridge. Not at the rate that Abingdon once turned them out, but 30 cars a day isn't to be sneezed at. These MGs are designed and assembled here but, because the big bits are made in China, the sale price can be kept very competitive indeed.

And if MG is about anything, it's fun at an affordable price. You can buy the funky little MG3 hatchback for just over £8,000, making it an ideal first car. Of course, it's perfect for squeezing into tight spaces – but not many people can park it the way that Paul Swift can.

Remember that James Bond film *Diamonds Are Forever*, where Bond tips a Ford Mustang up onto two wheels so he can escape down a narrow alleyway? Paul can do that all day long. His dad Russ ran a precision driving team and Paul was driving the family's ride-on lawnmower on two wheels when he was seven. And now he's going to show me how it's done in a Longbridge carpark.

Starting just a few feet away from a wooden ramp raised up on a couple of blocks, Paul gently accelerates the MG as I hang on to the grab handles. It all happens very quickly: one moment we're on level ground and the next we're tipped over at 45 degrees, me up top and Paul steering one-handed below me with his left arm wrapped around the back of my seat. He makes it look so easy!

After that, he lets me have a go at doing some handbrake turns. Although the MG3 puts out only 104bhp, it's really fun to whip around, and I'm thoroughly enjoying myself until I notice that Paul has started to turn slightly green and has gone a bit quiet. Turns out he's not a good passenger.

Riding in a car that's travelling on two wheels and at an angle of 45 degrees might sound scary, but I didn't feel remotely unsafe in the

OPPOSITE With the MG XPower SV – the car with the longest production line in the world. It finally ended the MG marque and bankrupted everybody involved with it. A bastard car.

RIGHT The new MG3 – built in Britain with Chinese money.

BELOW I want to see a two-seater MG, not a two–wheeler MG…

LEFT With John Wilson, MG racing team owner, at Silverstone.

BELOW We discuss race tactics – "Don't go out in the wet on these tyres," I say. But he disagrees, so I go out and spin out going in a straight line. What!

OPPOSITE The MGB GT V8 that I have to get the hang of on camera, in a race, in the wet. The scariest car I have ever raced. And no, I didn't get the hang of it.

little MG3. That's exactly the opposite of my experience at the wheel of the MGB GT V8 mentioned at the start of this chapter. It was one of the most frightening rides of my life.

Normally there's not much to be scared of in an MGB. It was the most popular MG ever made, with over half-a-million sold in the 1960s and '70s. Usually it came with a 1.8-litre motor and it's about as benign as the family labrador. The one I'm down to race at Silverstone has a 5.3-litre V8 putting out 420bhp, and it's a vicious pitbull of a car.

On my first lap around Silverstone, I glide around a corner as gracefully as a swan – and continue pirouetting onto the grass.

Right, that's it, I think: I'm going to do one lap and come into the pits for a set of rain tyres. But then, as I'm pulling about 70mph on the back straight – which is no kind of speed at all on a race track – the rear end snaps sideways and there's nothing I can do to catch it. I can see the trackside wall approaching rapidly and I just have to brace myself for the impact. Bang!

Fortunately, the damage is not severe and I'm able to drive back to the pits, where the owner's crew does a brilliant job of patching up the front end with gaffer tape and pop-riveted aluminium. We'll still be able to race.

I'll be honest. I really did not want to take that car out again. But I can't let everyone down, so when the time comes, I fire up that snarling V8 once more and head out onto the circuit. At first, nothing seems to gel. The car feels like it's working against me and we're not building a rapport. I'm even struggling with the straight-cut gears in the heavy-duty 'box.

Then something miraculous happens. The track has dried out and it no longer feels as though we're dancing on ice. Suddenly, the car and I have come together, and our lap times are dropping like a stone – I'm circling almost 40 seconds faster than I was at the beginning. This is more like it!

Alas, my triumph is short-lived – and so is my MG – because there's been an accident and the Safety Car is brought out. My team decides that now is the time for a driver change, so that we don't lose vital minutes later on. My race is over.

It's funny: I'm an adrenaline junky and I'm never happier than when I'm at the wheel of something sleek and powerful. Yet, even though my little 1954 MG TF wouldn't pull the skin off a rice pudding, I'd rather drive that any day than a 420bhp racing MGB that's on the wrong tyres. Power is nothing without control. And if it's not fun to drive, it's not an MG, in my book.

10 | MINI

A LONG-STANDING LOVE AFFAIR...

MINI

I bought my first Mini in 1967. White with a black roof, and I stuck GT stripes on it even though I didn't know what GT stood for back then (you can't imagine a car less suited as a Grand Tourer than a Mini). I also fitted wheel spacers to make the wheels stick out more, and all that did was to put lots of strain on the driveshaft joints and break them. But it looked cool.

Thing is, even though my Mini was only a bog-standard 850, it always felt fast. Until then I'd been trundling around in an old Ford Popular, bless it, which was an old man's car. I was young, and I was in a little rock 'n' roll band, and I could turn up at any party in the Mini and act like Jack the lad. The Mini suggested you were a little big naughty.

Which, of course, we were. The Mini was brilliant for courting. You could get in the back with your girlfriend, push the front seats forward and stick your ankles out of the sliding windows. At night, you'd see Minis bouncing up and down in car parks all over Whitley Bay and Tynemouth.

My love affair with the Mini never dwindled. When I first got married, we had a Minivan. We'd put the baby in the back and it would slide around merrily – no child seats in those days. But that little Minivan was a great everyday workhorse. When *Cars That Rock* was being mooted for a TV series, the Mini was the first car that came to mind, ahead of all the posh names like Bugatti and Ferrari and Rolls-Royce. And I wanted to talk not just about the cars, but about the people behind them.

BELOW A 1990 Mini Cooper with me and the irrepressible Paddy Hopkirk, laughing inside. I love Paddy.

OPPOSITE ABOVE The Mini production line in Oxford. Relentlessly clinical.

OPPOSITE BELOW Ian Cummings and I watch a new Mini roll by every minute and a half – about the same time as a stop at traffic lights.

> " **Owning a Mini suggested that you were above such concepts as having lots of money.** "

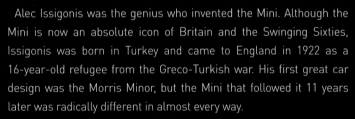

Alec Issigonis was the genius who invented the Mini. Although the Mini is now an absolute icon of Britain and the Swinging Sixties, Issigonis was born in Turkey and came to England in 1922 as a 16-year-old refugee from the Greco-Turkish war. His first great car design was the Morris Minor, but the Mini that followed it 11 years later was radically different in almost every way.

Remember that in 1959 Ford was still building cars like my sit-up-and-beg Popular, which had an archaic sidevalve engine and three-speed gearbox. The Mini had a peppy little 848cc overhead-valve unit and four-speed gearbox – but they were mounted sideways in the engine bay, to free up more space for passengers in the cabin. What's more, the engine and gearbox both shared the same sump for the oil, to save yet more space.

The Mini was therefore a brilliant piece of packaging, but it was successful not just because it was a 10ft-long box that could carry four people at 70mph. It was a hit because it was new and it was different. And, because it was an inexpensive car, it appealed to the ideals of the newly emerging classless society. Owning a Mini suggested that you were above such vulgar concepts as having lots of money.

Inevitably, therefore, it was the super-rich who took to the Mini in

their droves. All the Beatles had Minis. So too did Princess Margaret and Lord Snowdon, who were 'papped' leaving hospital in a Mini with their three-year-old son, David, Viscount Linley. The model Twiggy passed her driving test in her Mini, and so did "It Girl" Cathy McGowan, presenter of TV pop music show *Ready Steady Go!* Peter Sellers, a notorious petrolhead who bought cars like other people buy groceries, had his Mini customized by coachbuilder Hooper at a cost four times the price of the regular car. Even the Americans weren't immune: ultra-cool dudes such as James Garner and Steve McQueen – who were both keen racing drivers – had Minis with special paint jobs.

The Mini didn't just look cool, though. It had incredible handling because its tiny wheels were positioned at each corner of the car, it had a revolutionary kind of rubber suspension, and its little engine was very tunable. In souped-up Cooper specification it won the Monte Carlo Rally three times in 1964, '65 and '67 – and morally won the 1966 event, too, except that the dastardly French excluded it on a frivolous technicality, which just happened to let the second-placed Citroën move up into first.

These days, motorsport doesn't register much with the general public, unless it's Formula One. In the 1960s, however, the Monte Carlo

Rally was big news: when a Mini won it for the first time in '64, the winning car took pride of place on TV's *Sunday Night At The London Palladium*, which was as big then as *Strictly Come Dancing* is today (and Bruce Forsyth has presented both of them. That's amazing.) The man who drove it to victory in 1964, Paddy Hopkirk, received a telegram from the Prime Minister and a signed photograph from the Beatles with the handwritten annotation, "You're one of us now Paddy!"

I've seen that photograph myself, because it hangs in Paddy Hopkirk's loo in his sixteenth-century farmhouse in Buckinghamshire, and the first thing he did when I went to see him recently was to invite me into his toilet... "Oh aye," I said, "do you want to show me some puppies?"

But I've never met a warmer or more wonderful man. He charms you with his Northern Irish brogue and he's a national treasure; even if you're too young to remember his 1960s heyday in rallying, you'll have heard of Paddy Hopkirk Accessories, which have been available in all good motor factors for nearly half a century.

Paddy took me to a local airfield in the Mini that I'd turned up in, and I asked him to teach me how to do a handbrake turn. It was pouring with rain, which was good for encouraging the car to slide but bad in that we couldn't see a damn thing through the windscreen. The wipers were pathetic and it had started to steam up inside. "These demisters always were bloody useless!" exclaimed Paddy. We had such a lot

LEFT Paddy welcomes me to his country estate (and then takes me straight to the loo to see his telegram from the Beatles – thank God).

BELOW New and old Minis. Paddy drives both – which do you think he prefers?

OPPOSITE Paddy and I, having just graffiti-ed the Mini with our names.

of fun that day; I still have his phone number but I'm scared to call him because he's such a busy person and I don't want to bother him. That's how much I'm in awe of him.

Even before the Mini became a smash-hit in rallying, it had taken the race circuits by storm. Very early on, racing driver John Cooper had been lent a Mini for evaluation, and he happened to be campaigning in Formula Junior with a racing car that was powered by the same type of engine used in the Mini. He straightaway realized the Mini's potential, if it had more power and better brakes, and persuaded its makers – the British Motor Corporation – to let him make hotter versions and sell them as Mini-Coopers. The rest is history. The tiny Minis could out-

handle and out-corner just about anything on the racetrack, and the sight of them battling against huge American Ford V8s became the ultimate David-versus-Goliath spectacle in 1960s saloon car racing.

Although I've done lots of racing over the last two decades, I'd never driven a Mini in anger on a track, until I was invited to have a go in a race at Brands Hatch for the TV series. My steed would be a 1964 Mini-Cooper S, and I would be competing against a whole bunch of other Mini-Coopers and a handful of Ford Lotus-Cortinas, not to mention the odd BMW and Alfa Romeo.

Minis generally lose out against the bigger-engined cars on the straights but catch them in the twisty bits – and fortunately there are

plenty of twisty bits at Brands Hatch. I soon learned that the technique was to get my braking and downshifting done well ahead of the corner, and then just go balls-out on the inside line and not give quarter to anyone. Hurling this little car around the track was the most fabulous fun, but I still couldn't believe it when I finished sixth out of the eleven Minis in the race.

Driving a Mini again after all these years made me feel like a teenager. You don't so much sit in it as wear it, and with the upright driving position and the bus-like angle of the steering column it's like being inside a go-kart with a roof. I had such a ball that I persuaded the car's owner to sell it to me, like Victor Kiam in that old TV advert for Remington shavers, and I now keep it in the UK for racing in what are known as "historics".

Mini-Coopers are renowned among petrolheads for their racing antics, but to the man on the Sunderland omnibus they'll always be remembered for a certain film starring Michael Caine, Noel Coward and Benny Hill – yes, *The Italian Job*, in which red, white and blue Mini-Coopers went on the rampage on the streets (and pavements, and underpasses, and roofs) of Turin, in an attempt to steal a shipment of gold bullion from under the noses of the Mafia.

The British Leyland Motor Corporation, as BMC had become, was so strapped for cash in the late 1960s that they refused to supply any cars free of charge for the film, only grudgingly agreeing to sell six Minis at trade price and a further 30 at retail. None of them is known to have survived – there's a rumour that some were just pushed into an Italian lock-up and abandoned – but up in my native north-east of England three of the *Italian Job* Minis live on, thanks to a fanatical restoration by a Mini enthusiast called David Morton.

David is an amazingly clever guy. His day job is as Professor of Architecture at Northumbria University in Newcastle, and among his claims to fame is that he designed a self-build wooden house for Ikea. But his real passion is for Minis, and in particular the ones used in *The Italian Job*. When he heard that some remains of the original cars were coming up for auction, he and his wife remortgaged their house to buy them.

What they got for the £20,700 they had to pay at the sale was little more than a box of bits, plus the all-important vehicle logbooks and number plates. He then spent about 18 months rebuilding each car to immaculate condition, even enlisting the help of Sir Michael Caine (who signed the dashboards) and the film stunt organizer, Rémy Julienne. They are just perfect in every respect. David even tracked down the company that made the original jumpsuits worn by Charlie Croker and his gang in the film, and persuaded it to remake them.

Although the registrations on the Minis appear to be random collections of letters and numbers, each one has a story. Take HMP 729G, which is on the red car. "HMP" stands for Her Majesty's Prison, and "729" is Michael Caine's prison number in the film. Amazingly, the registrations had never been issued and David was able to buy them at a sale of cherished numbers, so that his Minis are legally registered as the cars from *The Italian Job*.

What I appreciated most was the way David and his wife reacted when I suggested that these Minis would probably fetch a quarter-of-a-million or more on the open market. Would they be tempted to sell them? They looked at each other, and both said, "No". Which as far as I'm concerned makes David the richest man in the world.

With the benefit of hindsight, it seems crazy that the bean counters at BLMC didn't realize the benefit of all the publicity they would get from the Mini-Cooper appearing in a big film. But back then, the company was in dire financial straits. Rival car maker Ford once took a Mini to pieces to work out how it could be sold for such a low price, and the answer was, it couldn't – every Mini cost £30 more to make than it's retail price.

As the 1960s turned into the '70s, it seemed as though the gloss was wearing off the Mini itself a little bit. The design was starting to look old rather than quirky, and then a whole generation of smart new hatchbacks like the Fiesta and the Golf began to appear. No one wanted Minis, least of all me; you always have a special affection for your first love and the Mk2 Minis and the ones that came after didn't have quite the same appeal.

It didn't help that cash-strapped British Leyland never had the money to invest in new engines or gearboxes, so the Mini always had to rely on its retro appeal to compensate for its shortcomings as a car. Thank God, then, for the Japanese, who kept buying them throughout the 1990s. Unbelievably, the last Mini wasn't built until October 2000, which was 41 years after the car had been launched.

By then, British Leyland had been through more changes of name than a schoolboy rock group, and in 1994 what was then known as Rover Group was bought by German giant BMW. They immediately set about designing a brand-new Mini for the twenty-first century, and it finally went on sale in 2001. Dubbed MINI to set it apart from the old car, it would have been more appropriately called Maxi, because it was much, much larger than the original. But that would have been stupid.

The MINI was unashamedly a pastiche of the original, but customers loved it, not least because they could choose from loads of options and order one that was different from any other on the road. Today, there's a mind-boggling 15 billion combinations available in several different body styles, and BMW's Oxford plant turns out 900 of them every day. Remember that, next time you're chatting someone up and can't think of what to say.

Be honest, though: if you saw an old Mini and a new MINI side by side, which would tug at your heartstrings? I'll lay good money that it's the old 'un. Of course it's nowhere near as well built or as pleasant to drive as the MINI. But it's got charisma in spades.

The good news is that while early Minis are now stupidly expensive, you can still pick up a late '60s or early '70s example for not very much money and you'll look like The Man because it's different. Or how about a Clubman in a really '70s colour like bright orange? Imagine how cool that would look driving through a city centre. But do it now, because in a few years' time they'll be worth a lot more.

Alec Issigonis, the man who started the legend back in 1959, never came up with anything quite as radical as the Mini ever again. Come to think of it, he probably did, but management would never have let him build it in a million years. He retired in 1971, and one of his retirement presents was a No.10 Meccano Set, the top-of-the-range one in the massive wooden cabinet. To quote a certain star from *The Italian Job*, "Not a lot of people know that".

OPPOSITE Me and another car that I met on this series while filming at Brands Hatch, and which won my heart completely. Dear reader, guess what I did next? I just had to buy it and race it.

RIGHT At Santa Pod, the fastest Mini in England – owned by Stuart Mead.

BELOW We go drag racing and Stuart lets rip ... and I swear a lot.

11 PORSCHE

CARS THAT ARE BUILT TO RACE

PORSCHE

> ## "It's just something about the 911. They're driven by bottom feeders and lawyers."

Brendan O'Brien, the producer of *Rock or Bust*, AC/DC's latest album, is a lovely guy. He's brilliant – he produces us, he produces Springsteen, he works with all the big names. But he's not a car guy. He drives a Prius and lives in Hollywood. I hate him. (I don't really, it's just that he drives a Prius.)

One day Brendan rings me up and announces that he's going to trade in the Prius for a Porsche. So he goes to the dealership and leaves in a new 911. He's driving down Sunset, heading for Malibu, and he's feeling like the King of the World. But then he notices people are looking at him, and not in a good way. "Brian, they were staring like I'd run over their dog," he told me later. "Then it dawned on me. I was The Guy In The Porsche. I couldn't stand it. I just turned around and headed back up Sunset and took the car back to the dealership."

I know how he felt, because I bought a 911 once. It was in 1985, a new Turbo with the huge picnic table spoiler on the back. Unlike Brendan, I lasted a week with that car. I took it to the pub and I could see everyone thinking, "Prat". It's not that they didn't like the car; in fact, they would have loved to have one themselves. It's just something about the 911. They're driven by bottom feeders and lawyers.

But I love Porsches. The 944 that I had before the 911 was one of the best cars I've ever owned. It looked stunning, even though it was in white and I thought I'd never have a white car. I was so happy I'd bought it instead of a 911. The salesman told me: "Of course, you know Mark Knopfler has just bought a 911." "Good," I told him. "I want that 944." I loved that car – so much so that I replaced it with another

ABOVE Porsche 911 Turbo. As owned by Brendan O'Brien and Brian Johnson. For a week.

OPPOSITE ABOVE I block the view of the Porsche production line in Stuttgart.

OPPOSITE BELOW Christian Will shows me what makes Porsche tick.

136

one a few years later. That was the S version, with the twin-cam head and 16 valves. I loved that one, too, until I lost it in the divorce. Well, shit happens.

The 911 is the car that everyone thinks about when you mention Porsche, because it's been in production in one form or other since 1963. But to understand what makes Porsche so special, you need to drive the model that came before it, the 356. It's the one that looks like an upturned bathtub and I was lucky enough to drive the open-top Speedster version when I visited the Porsche factory at Zuffenhausen, just outside Stuttgart.

I've got to admit, I was terribly impressed by the Porsche factory. I was impressed by the education of the workforce. They were intelligent people. I was impressed by their fanaticism, and I don't mean that in a bad way; they clearly believed in what they were making. I liked the way the workers are rotated between jobs, so they don't get bored, and I loved the fact that they are given a smoking break every hour, and the smoking rooms don't look like smoking rooms but like decent lounges, where you could spend time even if you don't smoke. Most of all, I like the fact that these cars are built by real people and not robots. The only robots are the ones that scoot around the factory delivering parts. That surprised me.

But while I enjoy a factory tour as much as the next man – that is, not very much – I much prefer driving, so I was pleased when they whisked me away to a place that is so secret, hardly any of Porsche's

employees even know about it. It's where they keep the Porsche museum's reserve collection, and if you like oddball and historic cars, it's better than Beaulieu. Would you believe they have an exact replica of a Porsche from 1900 – and it's a hybrid? There are electric motors in the front wheel hubs and two single-cylinder De Dion petrol engines to generate the electricity. Brendan O'Brien would love it.

The public wasn't quite ready for hybrid cars in 1900, however, and its designer, Ferdinand Porsche, didn't hit the big time until he came up with what, quite literally, was a People's Car, the Volkswagen, more than 30 years later. Unfortunately he fell in with a bad crowd – the Nazi party – and was imprisoned by the French after the Second World War. So his son, Ferry Porsche, set to using up some of those old VW parts to create a new sports car to raise money for Ferdinand's release.

That car was the 356 and it was launched in 1948. By the time the stripped-out Speedster appeared in 1954, it didn't have much in common with the old VW Beetle other than the fact it was still kind of Beetle-shaped and it had an air-cooled engine in the back. But it was beautifully built and it was a massive hit in America, where it was the exact opposite of the huge Cadillacs with their marshmallow handling.

These early 356s are not fast cars. The Speedster I drove is the stripped-out model, the one aimed at US customers who wanted to take it racing at the weekends. It has only 75bhp and it takes 14.5 seconds to reach 60mph from rest. That's more than four times as long as today's 911 Turbo S Cabriolet.

OPPOSITE ABOVE Their state-of-the-art production line. I still managed to get my hands dirty – see top right.

ABOVE We stroll on.

RIGHT We take a drive in a Porsche 356, Ferry Porsche's very own.

But to get hung up on the numbers is to miss the point. The 356 Speedster is a gorgeous little jewel of a car. It feels so tight, so together, and also so delicate. Because the weight of the engine is over the back wheels, the steering is beautifully light. You can practically think it into corners. And because the bath-tub shape is nice and slippery, that thrummy little flat-four can push it to well over 100mph. James Dean was a Porsche fan, and so was Steve McQueen. But then they were ugly buggers, so they needed all the help they could get in picking up girls.

Dean and McQueen (now there's a double act) were both serious racers, and that's why they liked Porsches. These cars are perfect for racing, because they're superbly made and they're reliable. It's been estimated that the company has won over 30,000 races all around the world, including 16 victories in the Le Mans 24 Hours – a record no other company can match. Steve McQueen even made a film called *Le Mans*, which begins with him driving to the circuit in a slate-grey 911. In the film he races arguably the greatest Porsche ever made: the 917.

The film uses footage from the actual 1970 Le Mans race, which was the first time Porsche won outright (although, ironically, it doesn't in the film, in which McQueen comes second to a Ferrari). What I really like is that one half of the team that delivered the victory that Porsche so craved was English. His name is Richard Attwood, and I met him at

THIS PAGE and **OPPOSITE**
Dieter Lendenberger takes me on a magical mystery tour of the secret Porsche storage facility somewhere in Germany.

Silverstone, where he had a rather special surprise lined up for me.

Richard is a very modest guy, but what he and his partner Hans Herrmann achieved in 1970 is truly heroic: 343 laps, 2,863 miles, at speeds of up to 240mph down the Mulsanne Straight. "There was a big party to celebrate afterwards, but I just could not stay awake," Richard confided. "I was completely wiped out!"

The real star of the show in the 1970 Le Mans was the Porsche 917. The car that won is worth maybe £30 million today, so the chances of someone like me being let loose in it are about the same as the Louvre museum inviting me to doodle on the Mona Lisa. But Richard had lined up an identical car for me to drive, which was

worth only a couple of million quid. So that's alright, then.

It's not the easiest car to get into – the racing safety harness is a bit tight around my gentleman's vegetables – but once you're in, it feels perfect. Fire up the 4.5-litre flat-12. *Heee-yarrr!* It's like the meanest, baddest kitchen food mixer you've ever heard, the cacophony of thrashing valves and pistons overlaid by the whir of the huge plastic fan on top of the engine – all Porsches were still air-cooled in those days.

Ease the 917 gingerly out onto the track. When the TV people laid down a soundtrack for this sequence in *Cars That Rock*, they chose Wagner's 'Ride of the Valkyries', and they were spot on, because this

ABOVE Stacks of great cars (literally). It was like a Pharoah's tomb, all the cars wrapped in white linen. An ethereal place.

LEFT A Porsche 917K, the 1970 Le Mans winner.

RIGHT The 1974 911 RSR belonging to my racing buddy, George Tuma. I love this car.

car is truly epic. Get it pointing in a straight line, goose the throttle and hold on tight ... *Whoa!* It's like sitting at the pointy end of a Messerschmitt 262 jet fighter. And this is the improved version, called the 917K ("K" for kurt, or short), which had a truncated rising tail to generate some downforce on the track. When the 917 first appeared in 1969, drivers were refusing to race them because they were practically taking off at high speed.

But the 917K is fabulous. It's so much better than I'd imagined it could be. Everything is right about it – the weight distribution, the position of the pedals, the brakes, and it's just so damn fast. I'll carry the memory of driving it with me forever.

They only made 65 Porsche 917s, but the die was cast. It was followed by what, to those who love Porsche, is a roll call of glory. The 935, the 956, the 962: they bestrode motor racing like giants. It's not only the purpose-built sports racers that could succeed on the racetrack, as I found out when I raced a 911 at Germany's infamous Nürburgring.

There are two circuits at the Nürburgring: the old Nordschleife, or North Circuit – nicknamed The Green Hell, after the woods that it runs through – and the modern Grand Prix circuit. They stopped holding F1 races on the Nordschleife after 1976, because it was so bloody dangerous. That last race was the one in which Niki Lauda crashed and burned in his Ferrari, and very nearly died.

Fortunately, I was to be racing on the modern circuit. The last time I was here was with AC/DC, when we played to 190,000 people. Now I'm about to drive a circuit that's incredibly challenging, where the regulars take no prisoners and wear knuckledusters over their driving gloves. I don't mind admitting, I'm nervous as hell.

But George's car looks unbelievably user-friendly, considering that it came fifth at Le Mans in 1975 – the highest-ever placing for a 911 in the 24 Hours. It's a 911 RSR, basically a pumped-up version of the 911 road car, with bigger brakes, wider wheels and more power. It even has a five-speed gearbox with synchromesh, and – get this – a key to start it. It looks too comfortable to be a race car.

So, George, any advice on how to drive it? "Stay longer on the gas, and shorter on the brakes!" Gee, thanks. We'll be going for class honours in the race, because we'll have no chance against the dedicated sports prototypes that will also be on track. The first day has been set aside for qualifying, with the race proper on the following day. George and I will each have one qualifying session and our grid position for the race will be averaged out from our respective lap times.

George goes out first, and I have everything crossed that he sets a good time, because it will take the pressure off me later in the day. But then, disaster: it starts to rain and the track becomes as slippery as a wet fish. Running on slick tyres, George loses it on a corner

ABOVE and LEFT George and I having a great day out at the races, despite the tricky conditions. It was very slippery, a bit like driving on fish.

and, while he recovers quickly from his spin, it's put us well down the running order.

A change of tyres, and I have just 30 minutes to claw back some time. The 911 has a reputation as being difficult to drive but incredibly rewarding to master, and I'm starting to feel that I'm getting to know this car. I even overtake somebody. At the end of the session, we finish 29th overall, which sounds terrible – but it turns out we're fifth in class. That's not so bad.

Race day dawns bright and sunny. Unfortunately, there's a problem with the car: the mechanics have told us we can't use fifth gear. That's a shame, because you normally use fifth quite a lot at the Nürburgring... But we decide to go out and race anyway. I'm as excited as if I'm about to go out on stage. Rock 'n' roll!

The plan is that I'll do the first stint and come in after 30 minutes to hand over to George. To start with, it's all going swimmingly and I'm moving up through the grid. Suddenly, bang! The engine in the car in front blows up and coats my windscreen with oil, and I can't see a thing. It's every driver's worst nightmare. I feel like a fighter pilot in the Battle of Britain who's been hit.

I have to head straight to the pits, where the crew cleans the windscreen as fast as they can, but I can feel valuable seconds slipping away. Back on the track, and I'm playing catch up. Just as I really feel like I'm getting to know this circuit, it's "Come in Johnson, your time is up!", Into the pits and it's over to George. But I'm still cursing my bad luck.

George is foot to the floor, and he knows this car and he knows this track, but it's still a Herculean task. With no fifth gear, we never really stand a chance of clawing back the time we lost. The spirits of drivers past just aren't with us today. But the important thing is that we have raced, we finished, and we lived to drive another day.

This one weekend has changed my mind about Porsches. I've always admired them, but now I've seen how you really can drive one to a track, stick a race number on it, have some fun and then take it to work again the next day. This is what they were built for. That's what I like about them: their Teutonic-ness. Is there such a word? Yes, there is, I've just made it up.

I love the 911. Forget what I said at the beginning of this chapter – if you've got a bit of money, go out and buy one. It doesn't matter whether it's old or new, they're all brilliant. Steve McQueen liked the one he drove at the beginning of *Le Mans* so much, he bought an identical car to use at home in California. What a git.

OPPOSITE I talk to the engine of our 911, in Geordie dialect, of course.

RIGHT I look longingly for.... the film crew. Must be lunchtime? Tip No.1: Never take a film crew for lunch or dinner. They can eat the arse out of an elephant.

BELOW A racing scene from the movie *Le Mans* (1971). Shown is Number 20, a 1970 Porsche 917K.

THE MOST ROCK 'N' ROLL CAR IN EXISTENCE

YCE

ROLLS-ROYCE

When I was little, my dad told me: "The only time you'll get to ride in a Rolls-Royce will be the day it's taking you to your funeral." He wasn't being nasty; it's just that the only Rolls-Royces we ever saw in our neighbourhood were hearses. The local undertakers used old pre-war Phantoms, which were big enough for them to get in without taking off their top hats – so, of course, to a small boy they always just looked enormous.

Well, it took me a while, but I finally got to own a Rolls-Royce. Not that I ever intended to. I've had lots of cars over the years, but never a Rolls-Royce. I sort of ended up buying one by accident. It's a Phantom, and it's the most rock 'n' roll car you can imagine.

I used to have a good buddy in Miami, who's now passed on, who was a Rolls and Bentley dealer all his life. One day he rings me up and says: "Brian, I've got something special for you." He then gives me this long story about a nearly new Rolls-Royce Phantom that he'd sold to a little old lady in Miami, but which turned out to be too big for her to handle. Then he'd remembered that I had a Bentley Continental GT, which would be perfect for her...

Now, I was very happy with my Bentley, although I'd only managed to put about 3,000 miles on it in two years because I was always away somewhere. So I tell him I'll think about it, and I ring off.

About 15 minutes later the door bell rings and there's a guy standing outside with a clipboard, and behind him is a huge covered wagon. "Mr Johnson? I have your new car." "What new car? I didn't order a new car." He opens the tailgate of the lorry and there's what looks like

BELOW Chauffeur School – Joe, our director, does his homework using a Rolls-Royce Silver Dawn as his desk.

OPPOSITE William Allan restores vintage Rollers in his garage near Chichester and is mad enough to let me drive an immaculate 1923 Silver Ghost.

> **" I never have a problem parking: every restaurant likes to have a Phantom out front. "**

a huge humpback whale in there. It's a Phantom, and when the guy pulls it out of the truck I can see that it's a deep, deep purple, almost black, and I fall in love there and then.

I call my dealer friend and I say: "You sneaky git! This was already on its way here when you called me!" But I took it for a drive anyway – and that was it. The acceleration was just stunning. It's not turbocharged, but the 6-litre V12 makes this two-and-a-half tonne monster move like manure off a shiny shovel. And yet it can turn like a London taxi – I couldn't believe it. I part-exchanged my Bentley there and then.

The Phantom and its smaller relation the Ghost are built at an amazing, hi-tech factory near Goodwood in Sussex. The money for the factory came from BMW, which has owned Rolls-Royce since 1998. Whatever you may think about this most British of British marques being owned by the Germans, it's a fact that Rolls-Royce is in the better shape now than it's been since the firm was founded. They make 15 cars a week at Goodwood – and what's more important, they sell them, too.

My Phantom is The Daddy of the range. It's not the fastest – though it sure feels fast – but it's the biggest and the most imposing. I never have a problem parking it outside restaurants in America. I pull up in front of the doors, and I ask the concierge where I should park, and they say: "No problem, sir. You can just leave it Right There." Every restaurant likes to have a Phantom out front.

The "small" Rolls-Royce is the Ghost, which in fact is also pretty big,

just not as big as the Phantom. It has the same V12 as the Phantom but with twin turbochargers, which push the power output to 560bhp and make it incredibly quick for something that looks like a housebrick but is actually the size of a small house.

More recently, Rolls-Royce launched the Wraith, which is a big two-door fastback coupé with an even more powerful version of the Ghost's V12. This is the Roller for rich people who like to drive themselves rather than let their chauffeur have all the fun. It has an eight-speed automatic gearbox that uses GPS to tell it when to change gear. Seriously. If you are coming down a steep mountain road and about to enter a hairpin bend, the GPS tells the gearbox to change down just ahead of it so it helps slow the car and save your brakes. That's clever.

Phantom, Ghost, Wraith – they're all great names from Rolls-Royce's history. Ghost has been around the longest; since 1906, when Charles Rolls and Henry Royce set out to create the very best car they could possibly make. It was painted silver and earned the nickname Silver Ghost, and if you're my age you probably remember the Corgi model of it from when you were a nipper.

Royce was the engineer in the partnership – he'd made his first car in 1904 – but Rolls was a Cambridge-educated posho who had the contacts necessary to sell the cars Royce designed. (Rolls was also mad keen not just on cars but on balloons and aircraft, and he would die in 1910 at the controls of a Wright Flyer monoplane. He was just 32 years old.)

Royce and Rolls decided to target the kind of wealthy buyers who might like a big car capable of transporting themselves, their family and all their luggage to their villas in the south of France or Tuscany. The Silver Ghost, which was launched in 1907, did not disappoint. It had a powerful 7-litre straight-six, and it was built with all the engineering skill that had given Britain an empire.

As a publicity stunt, the Silver Ghost was driven through England and Scotland for five weeks, covering 15,000 miles on some truly atrocious roads. At the end of the test, inspectors from the RAC ran their micrometers all over the car and found no detectable wear in any of the major components. Well, virtually none. They reported that one of the metal pins holding the rear springs to the chassis had worn by 0.0005in. That's one half of one-thousandth of an inch.

I had a chance to drive a Ghost when I visited classic car restorer William Allan in Sussex. He let me have a go in a 1921 example; they were built from 1907 to 1926 but didn't change very much in nearly two decades. Most of them didn't even come with brakes on the front wheels, which Rolls-Royce considered unnececessary – there was a worry that front-wheel brakes could provoke skids on the skinny tyres everyone used back then.

Front brakes are for girlies, anyway. More important is that the Ghost has a huge, whisper-quiet 7.5-litre engine, which is quite happy to pull the car along at any speed in top gear. In fact, in 2011, members of the 20-Ghost Club drove their vintage Ghosts from London to Edinburgh using only top gear, replicating another publicity stunt that Rolls-Royce had made 100 years earlier. And they didn't cheat, either: they followed the old country roads rather than motorways, and the gates for the gearchange were blanked off so that no-one could sneakily select a lower gear for moving off or going up a hill.

Ironically, though, the gearbox is a really nice thing to operate. You pull a lever that's the size of something you'd find in a railway signal box and it has that lovely, quality mechanical feel that the best cars of this era possess. There's another upright lever outside the car for the handbrake, which is useful for slowing the car down a bit as you approach a roundabout and change gear – you pull it on just a little and leave it on the ratchet, meanwhile changing down as you enter the roundabout, and then release it as you accelerate through, which means you don't have to bother with the footbrake (which also operates on the rear wheels) unless some thoughtless git in a modern tin box pulls across you at the last minute and you need to slam on the anchors. All part of the fun.

On the open road, you can easily cruise at 60–70mph in a Ghost of this vintage, which makes it perfect for long journeys – and, of course, you sit up as high as a Range Rover, only with rather more class. Hard to believe this car is close on a century old.

One thing that hasn't changed in all those years is the view over the front of the radiator when you're in the driving seat. The "Spirit of Ecstasy" mascot, which represents a young woman with arms outstretched and robes fluttering behind her like wings, has been fitted to nearly all Rolls-Royces since 1911 – and the story behind it is one of forbidden love and ultimate tragedy.

Most people associate Beaulieu in the New Forest, Hampshire, with the National Motor Museum; at least, they do if they're petrolheads. And the Second Baron Montagu of Beaulieu, John Douglas-Scott-Montagu, was one of the first proper petrolheads: a pioneer of the internal combustion engine, the first person to drive a motorcar into the House of Commons yard. Being an aristocrat, he could get away with that kind of outrageous behaviour.

OPPOSITE A new Wraith. Class motor. Stunning.

RIGHT Me and the lads on the shop floor of the Rolls–Royce factory.

What he couldn't get away with in the early 1900s – being an aristocrat – was marrying his mistress. She was his secretary and also the love of his life. Two problems: he was already married, and she was from 'below stairs'. Their relationship could never be made public. So John asked a sculptor friend of his, Charles Sykes, to make a mascot for his Rolls-Royce radiator, modelled after Eleanor Thornton, John's secretary and lover.

The very first mascots depicted Eleanor with a finger raised to her lips in a coquettish manner, hinting at a secret that couldn't be told. Then, when Sykes was commissioned to design a mascot that could be fitted to every new Rolls-Royce, he modified his original so that her arms were swept backwards, as if she were flying through the wind. She has done so ever since.

The tragedy is that John was posted to India in 1915, and the liner on which he and Eleanor were travelling was torpedoed by a U-boat. John survived after drifting for several days on a life raft, but Eleanor was drowned.

Just as it was unthinkable 100 years ago that John and Eleanor could have admitted their love for each other, it was equally unimaginable that someone from the lower orders – me, for example – could actually own a Rolls-Royce. Back in the day, they were driven only by

the very wealthy. Or rather, they weren't, because the very wealthy had chauffeurs to drive them. And some of them still do. Being a chauffeur requires particular talents, as I found out when I had a driving lesson from instructor Tony Fairley up in Newcastle, not far from where I grew up.

For one thing, Tony told me, a chauffeur must always walk around the back of the car to get to the driver's door, not the front. And if her Ladyship required assistance in exiting the motor vehicle, then it was permitted to extend a helping arm – but only with fist clenched, so there was not the slightest possibility of actually touching one's employer.

Tony put me through a chauffeur's driving test at the wheel of his own 1956 Rolls-Royce Silver Cloud, and I'm pleased to say that he complimented me on my wheel-handling skills. But then he added that he would have failed me for talking too much, since chauffeurs are supposed to be seen and not heard. And apparently it's not the done thing, when chauffering a bride to her wedding, to compliment her on having a fine set of knockers. Some people are so sensitive.

It was the arrival of rock 'n' roll and popular beat combos that finally saw what you might call the 'democratization' of Rolls-Royce, when people like me started to buy them. Pop stars, DJs and comedians all fancied being able to stare at Eleanor Thornton's nickel-plated

OPPOSITE Lord Montagu tells me the inside story of the Spirit Of Ecstasy, while his chauffeur drives us around Beaulieu in his 1914 Alpine Eagle. One of the most important and fascinating tales of automobilia.

RIGHT Fearon's wedding limos and chauffeur school in my home town of Newcastle. Alan is an old friend and used to look after my Bentley 8.

BELOW LEFT I have to take control of the film crew.

BELOW RIGHT Tony Fairley gives me a lesson – I appear to think I am doing OK.

backside; John Lennon cocked a snook at the establishment by having his Phantom V – one of the most expensive cars you could buy in the 1960s – painted in psychedelic colours.

This move towards popularizing the Rolls-Royce brand was helped by the arrival of the Silver Shadow in 1965. It was a genuinely modern car, built around a monocoque bodyshell rather than having a separate chassis, and it was a big seller – at least in Rolls-Royce terms. Nearly 30,000 of them were made up to 1980, which means that there are still plenty of them around. That is why you can buy a tatty but usable Rolls-Royce for as little as £2,000.

Drag racer Matthew Wright paid much less for his, however. He bought a 1974 Shadow for just 200 quid, and then threw most of it away. The bits he kept were incorporated into a dragster that can do 200mph and cover a quarter-mile at the drag strip in just six seconds. It's known as a "silhouette", because it looks like a Rolls-Royce from the outside, but underneath is a custom tubular-frame chassis and a very non-standard 9.5-litre twin-turbocharged Chevrolet V8 engine. And he took me for a ride in it down the Santa Pod drag strip.

Now, I've been in some pretty fast cars in my time – but this Roller puts out 1,600bhp at the wheels, all in one almighty rush, so it's trickier to handle than a spurned lover, and I was quite happy to leave the driving to Matthew this time. The massive Chevy V8 fires up with a noise like Zeus farting, and we rumble and grumble our way to the start line ready for a few seconds of death or glory.

First, Matthew spins the wheels up in the traditional drag strip burn-out, not just to entertain the crowd but mainly to get some heat into the huge rear tyres, so they will grip the track better. Then we wait for the signal to go.

The stop light turns from amber to green, Matthew floors the throttle, and young Eleanor leaps up and at 'em as the Rolls tries to pull a wheelie and lunges forward, Matthew calmly pulling a series of levers to shift the gears one-two-three-four as I get pinned back into my seat by the 747-like thrust of the V8 engine. And in less time than it takes to read that sentence, we've finished the run and Matthew has pulled the lever that deploys the parachute airbrake and I'm shaking with an adrenaline rush like I've never experienced before.

Drag racing is like that: a few seconds of intensity in between hours of preparation and waiting. The day I was at the drag strip, Matthew's car was parked up for hours in-between runs, and it was always surrounded by youngsters in hoodies taking pictures of it on their cameraphones. It seems that Rolls-Royce has the power to transcend class barriers and touch our hearts in such a way that, even if very few of us can afford to buy one, we all feel as though it's a part of our cultural heritage. Here endeth the lesson.

OPPOSITE Matthew Wright shows me the engine in his unique Rolls-Royce dragster at Santa Pod raceway, and he was so calm doing the Quarter Mile. I, on the other hand, wasn't.

RIGHT The usual style of drag cars, and something a little different.....

BELOW Matthew and I line up for the start.

ACKNOWLEDGEMENTS

So many wonderful people and characters made *Cars That Rock* possible. I'd like to thank Paddy Hopkirk, for example, who put me at ease during my first shot at presenting a TV programme. Closely followed by my family in Newcastle, for their excited phone calls after they'd watched the results.

Then there are all the car manufacturers who invited me to prowl their production lines and take a peek at their secret projects. George Tuma, my co-driver in Germany. Derek Bell, who taught me to drive with no hands. The brave lads from Race2Recovery. The very understated superstars of NASCAR, who showed true humility despite their greatness. There are too many to name, and I'm truly sorry that I can't single out every one of you.

I must pay tribute to the wonderful film and production crew from Back2Back for their patience whilst working with a complete beginner: Joe Scannell, Michael Nuvoletta, Emma Stamp, Archie Brooksbank, Doug Martin and Benedetta Pinelli – and, of course, Discovery Channel, for the loot to make it!

And last, but definitely not least, here's to Tarquin Gotch, my friend and manager, for believing that I could do this. Whether you were right or not is another matter, but bless you all the same.